THE FOUR GOSPELS

THE FOUR GOSPELS
THEIR LITERARY HISTORY AND
THEIR SPECIAL CHARACTERISTICS

BY THE REV.
MAURICE JONES, D.D.
RECTOR OF ROTHERFIELD PEPPARD, OXON
AUTHOR OF "THE NEW TESTAMENT IN THE TWENTIETH CENTURY"

WIPF & STOCK · Eugene, Oregon

Wipf and Stock Publishers
199 W 8th Ave, Suite 3
Eugene, OR 97401

The Four Gospels
Their Literacy History and Their Special Characters
By Jones, Maurice
Softcover ISBN-13: 978-1-7252-9742-5
Hardcover ISBN-13: 978-1-7252-9743-2
eBook ISBN-13: 978-1-7252-9744-9
Publication date 1/18/2021
Previously published by SPCK, 1921

This edition is a scanned facsimile of
the original edition published in 1921.

PREFACE

THE lectures contained in this volume were prepared for the "Training School for Clergy and Sunday School Teachers," organised by the Oxford Diocesan Sunday School Association, and held at Wantage in September 1919 and 1920, and were also utilised as the basis of a course of twenty-four lectures given to a Church Tutorial Class at Reading in the winter of 1919-20 The fact that the book had in view the needs of a particular audience accounts for the special character of its contents, and for the direct style and familiar tone that are frequently adopted in it. The lectures make no claim to originality of thought or treatment, but represent the attempt to set before a fairly well-instructed gathering of Clergy and Sunday School Teachers a general idea, in the light of recent research and within a well-defined compass, of the more important issues that arise from the study of the Gospels. I cherish the hope that what was found helpful by a body of Sunday School Teachers and by the members of a Church Tutorial Class, the majority of whom were engaged in secular teaching, may prove of value to that increasingly wide public which, although it does not contain many theological students in the strict sense of the term, is intensely interested in the study of the New Testament in general and of the Gospels in particular.

I desire to express my cordial thanks to my friend and neighbour, the Rev. H. Shears, M.A., of Peppard, who was kind enough to correct the proofs and to help me with many a useful suggestion.

MAURICE JONES.

The Rectory,
  Rotherfield Peppard.
    September, 1920

CONTENTS

	PAGE
LECTURE I	
THE GOSPELS	1
LECTURE II	
THE GOSPEL ACCORDING TO ST MARK	21
LECTURE III	
THE GOSPEL ACCORDING TO ST. MATTHEW	37
LECTURE IV	
THE GOSPEL ACCORDING TO ST. LUKE	59
LECTURE V	
THE GOSPEL ACCORDING TO ST JOHN	81
LECTURE VI	
THE GOSPEL ACCORDING TO ST. JOHN—*continued*	103

BIBLIOGRAPHY

E H Askwith, *The Historical Value of the Fourth Gospel*, 1909
B W Bacon, *The Beginnings of the Gospel Story*, 1909
E R Buckley, *Introduction to the Synoptic Problem*, 1911
F C Burkitt, *The Gospel History and its Transmission*, 1906.
—— *The Earliest Sources of the Life of Jesus*, 1910
J Estlin Carpenter, *The First Three Gospels*, 1904
J R Cohu, *The Gospels in the Light of Modern Research*, 1909.
C Gore, *The Epistles of St. John (Introduction)*, 1920
W W. Holdsworth, *Gospel Origins*, 1913
H Scott Holland, *The Philosophy of Faith and the Fourth Gospel*, 1920
H L Jackson, *The Problem of the Fourth Gospel*, 1918
A Menzies, *The Earliest Gospel*, 1901
C F Nolloth, *The Rise of the Christian Religion*, 1917
J Armitage Robinson, *The Study of the Gospels*, 1903
—— *The Historical Character of the Fourth Gospel*, 1908
W Sanday, *The Criticism of the Fourth Gospel*, 1905
E F Scott, *The Fourth Gospel, its Purpose and Theology*, 1909
—— *The Historical and Religious Value of the Fourth Gospel*, 1910.
J M. Thompson, *The Synoptic Gospels*, 1910.
J M Wilson, *The Origins and Aims of the Four Gospels*, 1910.

THE FOUR GOSPELS

THEIR MUTUAL RELATIONSHIPS AND THEIR SPECIAL CHARACTERISTICS

LECTURE I

THE GOSPELS

I *The attraction of the Gospels.*

IN an age when reading is no longer the privilege of the few and books are the happy possession of the many it is gratifying, and perhaps not a little surprising, to find that the Gospels of the New Testament still retain their pride of place in the affections of those who read. The attraction of the Gospels is proved not only by the countless numbers of the documents themselves which are sold, but even more by the large output of books year by year, which have the Gospels and their contents as their subject. The fact that books of this description are published in considerable profusion implies a corresponding demand and is proof positive that there does exist in the reading public of our day, and in every section of it, an increasing desire to acquire a more intelligent and a more scientific understanding of the Gospels and what they contain, and a more living realisation of the value of what the Gospels have to teach Some of the interest manifested in the Gospels is doubtless due to their qualities as pure literature, there is to the mind that has been trained to appreciate what is noble and beautiful in letters an irresistible charm in the simplicity of their language, in the purity of their style, in their matchless art of telling a story, and in the living force of every portrait they contain

But it is not as literature and literature only that the Gospels make their appeal to and are read by the masses, and the true explanation of their attraction must be sought in another and more profound direction than this. At no period in the history of Christianity has attention been so concentrated on our Lord Jesus Christ as in the modern world, never has He or His work made such a wide appeal as in the age in which we live There is in the present day a deeper consciousness of what He means and of what His teaching stands for in history and progress than has ever been felt before To quote a modern writer, "Amidst the crumbling of old forms and institutions, when that new order is dawning for which one and all hope but which no one may as yet discern, the gaze is riveted on Jesus with an intensity hitherto unknown. That precisely at this juncture He has some word for us and we great need of Him is not so much an intellectual perception as a profound consciousness which is overwhelming for the inmost soul."[1] To put the matter briefly, the question "What think ye of Christ ?" is being incessantly asked and with increasingly insistent force, and it is in the demand for an adequate response to this question that we find the real explanation of the attractive power of the Gospels upon the more thoughtful and more earnest minds of our day. The higher and truer appreciation of the place of Christ in the life of to-day has created a

[1] Carl Holliday, *Hibbert Journal*, xv p. 302.

THE GOSPELS 3

burning desire to penetrate beyond the ages that separate His historical life upon earth from our own world, to pass behind the whole mass of Christian literature that was the outcome of His coming, to get into living touch with the original authorities and to learn from these, at first hand as it were, what impression He left upon the world He moved in and upon the men with whom He lived in familiar intercourse. It is this craving to come into actual contact with the very fountain-head of truth that explains the cry now so frequently heard on the lips of religion, " Back to Jesus " There is in the hearts of men a longing not only to have the earliest and simplest picture of our Lord as He lived in the days of His flesh and moved among men, speaking and teaching and working, to learn how He died and rose again, but also to know what was the attitude of the Founder of Christianity towards life, what were His ideas concerning God and man, and in particular, to have this knowledge set down in His own words and in His own accents.

It is true, doubtless, that the interest taken in the Gospels by the present generation is not exclusively based on a genuine reverence for the Person and teaching of Jesus Christ, and that there are many who read and study them diligently with the deliberate view of defacing or removing the impression He has made upon the world, were such an achievement possible. But it may be said even of hostile criticism that it has proved a blessing to the cause of religion, inasmuch as it has been the means of encouraging among Christians generally a more thorough, intelligent, and scientific study of the Gospels and has, therefore, been productive of the most beneficial results in the sphere of New Testament research. But it is not hostility but a real friendliness towards the Person of Our Lord and His teaching that explains the increasing attraction of the Gospels for the mass of thinking humanity The world of to-day longs to know Him better.

II. *Why and how the Gospels came into being*

The word "gospel" does not now possess the meaning it once had in Greek literature or even in the New Testament itself Εὐαγγέλιον was originally employed to denote the "reward given to the bearer of good news" and from this it gradually came to mean the "good news" itself. It is in this sense that it is used in our Gospels, where it generally stands for the "good news of the coming of the Kingdom of God or of the Messiah." When St. Paul in Rom. ii. 16 speaks of "my gospel," what he has in mind is the sum of Christian teaching which it was his function to carry through the world. It was not until a generation or two of Christians had passed away that the term came to be applied to describe a certain kind of book, a book containing the original "gospel" taught by Christ and preached by His Apostles in a written form. A similar development marked the history of the correlative term "evangelist." In Apostolic days, as we see from Ephes iv. 11, the term was the title of a regular class of teachers who devoted themselves to the spreading of the "good news," and it was not until much later that it came to denote the author of a written Gospel

When the documents that now compose the New Testament began to be collected and to be formed into one united whole the first four books constituted one group designated "The Gospel," and each member of this group was regarded as giving a distinct representation of this Gospel, as we see from the titles which eventually were attached to them, "the Gospel according to St Matthew," etc. These titles did not belong to the Gospels originally and did not emanate from the

THE GOSPELS

Evangelists themselves. The Gospels were all published anonymously, and it is not until towards the end of the second century that we meet with the actual names of the Evangelists in the writings of Irenæus, and afterwards in those of Clement of Alexandria and Tertullian at the beginning of the third century.

There never was a time in the history of the Christian Church when she was not in possession of her Sacred Scriptures, but it was not the New Testament that was in her hands when she made her first approach to the world The Bible of the Apostolic Church was the Bible of the Jew, the Old Testament Scriptures, and in the Greek and not the Hebrew version The Church, however, was never without her " gospel," in the earlier meaning of that term, denoting, as explained above, the good news of the coming of Christ into the world and of redemption through His Cross and Passion. What the first generation of Christians did not possess was a " Gospel" in our sense of the term, i e an authoritative and written record of the story of our Lord's life and ministry, or a transcript of His teaching The " gospel" of that age was an oral gospel, the gospel as it was preached and taught by missionaries like St. Peter and St. Paul. But this gospel which was delivered by the missionary by word of mouth did not differ materially from the written Gospel which is in our hands to-day. Then as now it was a message of a new Life, a new Gift, and a new Hope The gospel of those days included at the least the main events in the ministry of our Lord from the Baptism to the Ascension, and at that time, as St. Paul's Epistles plainly show, the Death and Resurrection were as strongly accentuated as they are in the Gospels of the New Testament. Great stress was also laid by the Apostolic teachers upon the inseparable connection between the Old and New

6 THE FOUR GOSPELS

Dispensations and, in particular, upon the way in which the Messianic prophecies of the Old Testament were realised in Christ. This type of teaching must have drawn attention to the genealogy and earthly descent of Christ and would demand the telling of the story of His birth and of His early surroundings The teaching of Christ would also inevitably be in constant request as the final authority in all matters of controversy and as the solvent of the many practical difficulties with which the Christian missionary would be faced in the course of his travels We may, therefore, assume that this oral gospel, which was practically all that the Church was possessed of in the earliest stage of her history, was in its general character not unlike the gospel that was eventually committed to writing It told the story of our Lord Jesus Christ from the day of the Annunciation to the day of Ascension, and no important aspect of His life, work, and character was ignored The itinerant preacher would tell of Christ the Teacher and what He taught, of Christ crucified and risen, of Christ living in the believer, of Christ soon to come again, of Christ the herald of a new world.[1]

It is not easy for us to understand how or why the Church could have allowed any substantial period of time to elapse before she took in hand the provision of a written Gospel. Why did not the Church guard the interests of posterity by reducing the gospel story to a permanent and indestructible form at the earliest possible moment? Why allow the risk to be run that any word which fell from the Master's lips should fall into oblivion and be lost or that any one event in His life should be forgotten? There are, as a matter of fact, several reasons which explain the inaction of the early Church in this matter. First of all there was a strong prejudice among

[1] Cf. Wilson, *Origin and Aims of the Four Gospels*, p 8.

THE GOSPELS

Jews of that period against committing oral teaching to paper Although the Rabbis had piled up a mountain of oral law none of it was allowed to take a written form. " Commit nothing to writing " was a well-known maxim of the Rabbinical Schools [1] And again we must bear in mind that for the earliest generation of Christians there was no posterity whose interests it was necessary to protect, and no future on earth for the Church For them the end of the ages was close at hand, at the very door, and the day would soon dawn when the Son of God would appear in glory to usher in His Kingdom and to reign with His saints for ever That the Church was to exist upon earth for ages untold was an idea that was absolutely alien to the mind of primitive Christianity, and we can now realise why the existence of the gospel story in a written form did not present itself to the Church of that day as an immediate and fundamental necessity The life of the world was rapidly drawing to its close and, in the meantime, the words and works of the Master were so indelibly printed on the hearts and minds of the Christian disciples that it was unthinkable that any single item could be lost in the few years of existence still in store for the Church And besides had they not with them the eye-witnesses, those who had lived and walked with Jesus, men and women whose very existences were living evidence of the life and teaching of the Master ? Why trouble to write Gospels for a posterity that would never arise, when you had disciples of the Lord still around and among you, with every word and look of the Lord burnt into their memories ?

But as the years rolled on a change came over the situation The Christians of the Apostolic age now began to realise that the end was not as imminent as

[1] Carpenter, *The First Three Gospels*, p. 17.

they had imagined it to be and to understand that the Church, in the providence of God, would have to face the world in the generations to come Again, the circle of Apostles and eye-witnesses was diminishing day by day, and the time would soon arrive when the very last of them would be called away and the Church left without a single witness whose evidence was unimpeachable. And lastly, heresy and false doctrine were already beginning to make their presence felt in the Church. There was now, therefore, every reason why the Church should be supplied with the gospel in an authoritative, authenticated, and imperishable form Troublous times were ahead of her, and if the gospel of Jesus Christ was to be preserved in its original purity and truth it was imperative that it should be committed to writing without further delay.

How the demand arose among the early Christians for a written gospel and how that demand was responded to is well illustrated by a quotation from the writings of Clement of Alexandria which is found in the Ecclesiastical History of Eusebius. Clement is discussing how the Gospel of St. Mark came to be written, and he remarks: "When Peter was preaching the gospel in Rome many of those present besought Mark, his intimate companion, to commit to writing all that Peter said and so compose a Gospel and give it to those who asked for it When Peter was informed of the proposal he neither encouraged it nor forbade it" (Eus., *H E.*, vi. 14).

St Mark accepted the task imposed upon him, although Clement's language seems to imply that the congregations were more anxious to be supplied with a written Gospel than the Apostle to provide it. It would appear from this extract that it was the Christian laity and not the hierarchy that was the first to feel the need of the Gospel in a written and permanent form,

THE GOSPELS

and that it was owing to the initiative of a Christian congregation at Rome that that desire was translated into action The incident related by Clement may not be absolutely historical, but it does serve to illustrate how Clement thought that the movement was set on foot to convert a gospel that had hitherto been handed down by word of mouth, the authenticity of which had depended upon the accuracy of memory, into a written document

III. *The Gospels of the New Testament*

It is unquestionable that there must have existed at one time in the Church other Gospels or records of our Lord's life and teaching besides those that have come down to us in the New Testament. The New Testament itself is proof that the Apostolic age was essentially a literary age, when documents of various descriptions were in great request, and the definite statement in the prologue of St Luke that "many have taken in hand to draw up a narrative concerning those matters which have been fulfilled among us" (1 1) implies that when the Evangelist undertook the task of writing there must have been in existence several attempts of that character besides the Gospels now associated with the names of St. Matthew and St. Mark. The history of these early efforts is wrapped in obscurity Some no doubt disappeared after a brief and inglorious existence, some were utilised and incorporated in our canonical Gospels, and were, therefore, set aside and perished, and, except as far as they are embodied in the New Testament, have left no trace of their existence. Of Gospels of later origin than the Gospels of the New Testament, the uncanonical or Apocryphal Gospels as they are called, many specimens have come down to us, but as a rule only in a fragmentary condition. Thus we have Gospels of Peter, of James, of Matthias, of Thomas, of Philip and many others, some of them deliberately put together in order to propagate heretical doctrines by the adaptation of one or more of the canonical Gospels to the tenets of a sect or party on the borders of the Catholic Church, and others written to meet the needs of popular Christianity by supplementing rather than rivalling the canonical Gospels. In no instance has the Church shown her wisdom and inspiration more clearly than in her refusal to grant to these imaginative and often grotesque compilations a place among her canonical Scriptures. A mere glance at the Apocryphal Gospels enables us to realise the impassable gulf separating them from the New Testament Gospels and to understand why they were so ruthlessly condemned by the Catholic Church. The Gospels of the New Testament have survived simply because they deserved to, and their place among the Scriptures of the Catholic Church is due entirely to their qualities. Other Gospels have perished or been rejected because the inspired judgment of the Church failed to find in them anything of real religious or historical value.[1]

IV *The Synoptic Problem*, or, What are the relationships existing between the first three Gospels?

The four Gospels can be divided into two well-defined groups, the one comprising *St. Matthew*, *St. Mark*, and *St. Luke* and the other *St John*. To the first group it is now customary to give the title of "Synoptic Gospels," because they present the same general outlook upon the events recorded in them. They relate, in a measure, the same incidents, they give a similar impression of

---

[1] See Armitage Robinson, *The Study of the Gospels*, p 4.

THE GOSPELS

our Lord's Person and activity, and possess a remarkable unity in their view of the history of Christian origins. This unity of outlook and plan characteristic of the three Gospels is, however, combined with a considerable variety in detail, and we shall have much to say later concerning those features which are peculiar to each individual Gospel. The fourth Gospel stands in a class by itself and will be dealt with separately.

One of the greatest achievements of New Testament criticism in recent years has been the discovery of the real relationship that exists between the first three Gospels, regarded as literary documents. That some kind of connection did exist between the three has been recognised from the earliest days, because of the very striking similarity between them in language and contents, and until quite recent times this homogeneity was explained by what was called the "oral theory" According to this hypothesis the gospel record, while it was still being handed down from mouth to mouth, had become so fixed and stereotyped by constant repetition and the use of the catechetical method that there existed in the early Church a "gospel" whose terms and content were to all intents and purposes as well and as accurately defined as if that "gospel" had been actually committed to writing In support of this theory considerable stress used to be laid upon the abnormal cultivation of the memory in the East in all ages, an apt illustration of which is found in the present day in the practice among Mohammedan children of learning long sections of the Koran by heart, and it was thought that this unusual development of the faculty of memory was adequate to account for the fixity and accuracy of the gospel tradition. It was this "oral gospel," then, with its assumed fixed and stereotyped character, that was regarded as forming the basis of our

THE FOUR GOSPELS

first three Gospels and as explaining the manifest likeness that existed between them. This was the view of no less an authority than Bishop Westcott, but it has now been abandoned by the great majority of New Testament scholars, although one or two strenuous supporters of the theory are still to be found It is being increasingly felt that the "oral" theory fails to give an adequate explanation of the salient factors which constitute the Synoptic problem, and that although it might account fairly satisfactorily for the coincidences it breaks down when faced with the divergences.

Dr. Burkitt, in his fascinating book *The Gospel History and its Transmission* (chap 11), points out that if the primitive source had been a fixed oral tradition the incidents identically related in all three Gospels would certainly have been the central points in the Ministry and not a critical selection of anecdotes But it is precisely in the record of such events as the Institution of the Eucharist, the Words from the Cross, and the story of the Resurrection that we find the greatest variations, whereas in such small and trivial particulars as the command "Arise" in the story of the healing of the paralytic, and Herod's alarm about Jesus, there is the most complete agreement between the three Evangelists. Dr. Burkitt further remarks that if there had existed an "oral" gospel which was fixed and definite in its terms, as the hypothesis we are discussing demands, it would have been so authoritative that the Evangelists would not have ventured to treat it with the freedom which the Gospels exhibit. A documentary source, on the other hand, is definite but not necessarily authoritative, and can be handled with tolerable freedom by those who employ it It is not too much to say, therefore, that the "oral" hypothesis has had its day

THE GOSPELS 13

and must now resign in favour of the theory which postulates that the close connection between the Synoptic Gospels is based on the use of *written sources* by the Evangelists. It would be out of place in a course of lectures of this character to attempt to deal in detail with the many factors which constitute the Synoptic Problem, and we must be content with drawing attention to two or three of the main results which recent research may be said to have established.

(a) *The priority of St. Mark* —It may now be accepted as proved almost beyond question that *St Mark* is the oldest of the New Testament Gospels, although a scholar here and there still clings to the old idea that *St Matthew* was the first in point of time as it is first in order of place in the New Testament. The reason why the priority of *St. Mark* is now so positively held is that a scientific analysis of the Synoptic Gospels shows clearly that a copy of our second Gospel was actually in the hands of the authors of the other two, that they embodied it almost entirely in their own compositions, and that they used St. Mark's plan as the framework in which they incorporated his Gospel as well as other material collected from various sources. I will not detain you by attempting to give a detailed proof of this statement, beyond stating that a study of these three Gospels in any modern "Synopsis" such as Thompson's *The Synoptic Gospels* will go far to convince you that there is one document common to all three Gospels and that *St. Mark* is the document in question. It is quite possible that there were more editions than one of this Gospel current in the Apostolic age and that the versions used by St Matthew and St. Luke were not exactly identical. Some scholars suggest that the version in possession of St. Matthew was later than that used by St. Luke, while our canonical *St. Mark* represents a still later edition of the original Marcan document. This may account for the variations in matters of detail which are found in the narratives of identical incidents in the different Gospels.

(b) *A second Evangelistic source called Q* —The same method of research that discovered that *St Mark* is our original and earliest Gospel also brought to light another fact of equal importance. A careful comparison between *St. Matthew* and *St. Luke* showed that the authors of these two Gospels had not only used *St. Mark* and incorporated it in their own compositions, but that another and a second written source had been utilised by these two Evangelists. *St Mark* is in the main a narrative of incidents in our Lord's life and contains but little of His teaching, but this second document would seem to have consisted chiefly of His sayings and discourses It is generally designated by the letter "Q" (from the German "quelle" = source). Many authorities maintain that it is identical with a document referred to in a statement by Papias, an ecclesiastical writer of the middle of the second century, which is quoted by Eusebius (*H. E* , III. 39) "So then Matthew composed the *logia* in the Hebrew language, and each one interpreted (*or* translated) them as he was able." It is only right, however, to state that there is a growing body of opinion which refuses to see in the "logia" of Matthew anything resembling the character of Q and holds that these were not Christian excerpts at all, but a collection of Old Testament passages which was used by Christian missionaries and preachers in order to confirm the truth of the Christian gospel. If, however, the document mentioned by Papias in the above extract and what we now call Q are really identical we should then understand why the first Gospel (if not actually the work of that Apostle) was attributed to St. Matthew, the

THE GOSPELS 15

reason being that the original Matthæan document was embodied in this Gospel with particular completeness.

It is practically impossible to account for the extraordinary linguistic resemblances between the representations of our Lord's teaching as given in St Matthew and St Luke respectively, without assuming the use of some such document as Q on the part of the two Evangelists. We cannot, however, arrive at anything like a precise estimate of the contents of Q nor can we define its exact limits. We have *St. Mark* before us and we can, therefore, tell exactly how it has been dealt with by the other Evangelists, but this comparison is not possible in the case of Q, as the original document has been lost. Most of our leading New Testament scholars, both here and on the Continent, have tried their hands at reconstructing Q, and Moffatt in his *Introduction to the Literature of the New Testament* gives an analysis of sixteen of these efforts, no two of which are in anything like exact agreement with one another. The great majority of these schemes are drawn up on the principle of including in Q all the non-Marcan material which is common to the two Gospels, but even so there is a conspicuous lack of harmony among them. In the matter of this second Evangelistic source, then, it would seem that we must rest content with assuming that some early record of our Lord's sayings and teaching did lie before our first and third Evangelists, while keeping an open mind as to what this record actually contained.

The broad results of recent inquiry into the nature of the connection existing between the Synoptic Gospels may be summarised as follows :

(1) The similarity between these three Gospels in language and contents is based not upon a traditional "oral" gospel, but upon the use of documentary sources.

(2) The Gospel of St Mark is the earliest of the three.

THE FOUR GOSPELS

(3) St. Matthew and St. Luke have utilised St. Mark's Gospel as a framework for their own Gospels and have borrowed practically the whole of it.

(4) These two Evangelists have also employed a second document generally designated Q, which seems to have been mainly a record of the sayings and teaching of our Lord. The precise contents and limits of this document cannot be defined with any precision.

V. *When were the Gospels written ?*

There was a time soon after the middle of the nineteenth century when advanced criticism made desperate efforts to prove that all the four Gospels were the product of the second and not of the first century, and could not, therefore, be credited with the unimpeachable authority which is attached to writings that belong unquestionably to the historical period they profess to describe. This phase of New Testament criticism has happily had its day and there are now comparatively few scholars of rank who are prepared to place the Gospels as a body outside the first century, or to deny that the Synoptic Gospels were in existence prior to the year A.D. 80.

Now this change of attitude towards the dates of the Gospels is a gain of considerable significance. The all-important point in this connection is not whether, *e. g* , St. Mark and St. Luke were the authors of the Gospels attributed to them, although there is no sound reason for questioning this hypothesis in either case, but whether the authors of these Gospels belonged to the age they claim to describe, which would of course be true if the Gospels were written before the year 80. The Evangelists would then have lived and consorted with those who were eye-witnesses of the events they relate, even if they had not been eye-witnesses themselves, and would have had behind them the authority

THE GOSPELS

and witness of the Apostolic founders of the Christian Church. But there is a tendency among scholars in the present day to bring the composition of the Gospels much nearer to the life of our Lord and to the events they describe than the year 80, and to place the writing of the Synoptic Gospels not between A D 65 and 80 but between A D. 45 and 65 The great German scholar, Harnack, is primarily responsible for this movement. He bases his conclusions almost entirely upon the assumption that the *Acts* must have been written before the death of St Paul, the more general opinion being that St. Luke composed the Acts some fifteen or twenty years later than St Paul's martyrdom, *i. e* somewhere between A D. 80 and 90. Harnack insists that the reason why this book closes so abruptly and unsatisfactorily is that St. Luke must have died towards the close of the two years the Apostle spent in " his own hired dwelling," and had, therefore, no opportunity of completing his narrative and of ending it with the story of St. Paul's trial and death at Rome. Now if the *Acts* was in being before the close of St Paul's first imprisonment (A.D. 62), two conclusions follow On his own confession in Acts 1 1 St Luke had completed his Gospel before he undertook the further task of writing the *Acts*, so that if the latter was in existence in 62 we may quite reasonably place the writing of the Gospel before A D 60. Again, St Luke had a copy of St. Mark's Gospel before him when he was composing his own, so that our second Gospel was presumably written early in the decade which began with the year 50. Archdeacon Allen [1] goes even further than Harnack in this direction and maintains that *St. Mark* in an Aramaic version existed as early as the year 44, that it was current in a Greek form before the year 50 and that

[1] Allen and Grensted, *Introduction to the New Testament.*

THE FOUR GOSPELS

St. Luke had composed his Gospel before 58. Mr Edmundson in his Bampton Lectures, *The Church of Rome in the First Century*, dates the two documents as follows: *St Mark*, 44-45, *St. Luke*, 58-59 (*Acts* before 62), and Dr Nolloth[1] is of opinion that all the three Synoptic Gospels were current before the year 60. I must confess that I am not convinced of the soundness of dating *St Matthew* and *St. Luke* earlier than the year 60 and mainly for two reasons First of all the *Acts*, to my mind, points irresistibly to the conclusion that St. Paul was dead when it was written, and secondly there seem to be strong indications in both Gospels that the destruction of Jerusalem was already a thing of the past and that consequently they could not have been written before the year 70 But the dates of the two documents which mainly underlie these two Gospels, viz. *St. Mark* and Q, stand on quite a different footing. It is quite possible that the earliest version of *St. Mark*, perhaps in an Aramaic form, was current not much later than A D. 45 The Evangelist himself was evidently in close intercourse with St Peter when that Apostle was arrested by Herod in 44, because his mother's house was the place of assembly of the Christian congregation in Jerusalem at that time, and there is nothing improbable in the supposition that he then began to make notes of the Apostle's preaching and that out of these early notes the first draft of his Gospel was made The tradition handed down by Clement of Alexandria to which I have previously referred (p 8) would then have to do with the Greek version of the Gospel which was published somewhat later in Rome Again, Q is now generally recognised as our earliest Gospel source, and it has been suggested that in its primitive form it may belong to the period of our Lord's Ministry and

[1] Nolloth, *The Rise of the Christian Religion*, p 19

THE GOSPELS

be an actual transcript of our Lord's teaching taken down at the time by the Apostle, St Matthew. The document apparently stopped short before the Passion, which may mean that it was complete when that event took place Thus, although we may not be justified in placing the writing of our first and third Gospels before the year 70, we may without any undue stretch of the imagination bring the earliest Evangelistic sources very much nearer to our Lord's lifetime The date of St. John's Gospel will be dealt with when we come to study that Gospel, but we may remark here that recent criticism on that point shows a gratifying tendency and that the view of the Tubingen school which relegated the Gospel to the middle of the second century has now been almost entirely abandoned. The Gospels, then, as a body may be confidently claimed as the product of the first century and as documents whose authenticity and trustworthiness are founded on the evidence of men who, if not themselves eye-witnesses, had lived in intimate fellowship with those who had lived and walked with Jesus This, as I have already remarked, is the factor that is of supreme importance in this connection.

VI *The order of the Gospels in the New Testament.*

It may be interesting at this point to say something concerning the order in which the Gospels are placed in the different groups of New Testament MSS now in our possession. In the earliest Greek MSS the order is identical with that which obtains in our New Testaments, viz. *St Matthew, St Mark, St. Luke, St John*, but in the Versions (*i. e.* translations from the original Greek into other languages, Latin, Syriac, etc.) a different order prevails, viz *St. Matthew, St John, St. Luke, St. Mark* In the former of the two lists priority is based on the supposed ages of the Gospels, *St. Matthew* being taken as the earliest and *St. John* as the latest of the four. In the second list, however, there is another principle at work. *St Matthew* and *St John* are placed in front because they were written by *Apostles*, *St. Luke* and *St Mark* follow because they were the work of *Apostolic men*, and not of Apostles in the strict sense of the term It will be noticed that *St. Mark* is placed in a somewhat obscure position in both lists, behind *St. Matthew* in the first and behind *St. Luke* in the second. This no doubt reflects the opinion of the early Church as to the relative inferiority of *St. Mark* as compared with the other three Gospels.

Tradition assigned to each Gospel an appropriate symbol, corresponding to the four Cherubim in Ezek 1 10 and the four Living Creatures of Rev. iv. 7, viz the Man, the Eagle, the Lion, and the Calf. As a rule the Man was assigned to St. Matthew, the Eagle to St. John, the Calf to St. Luke, but each one of the four symbols has been assigned to St. Mark by different writers, although the connection of the Lion with St. Mark has been stereotyped in the world of art.

LECTURE II

THE GOSPEL ACCORDING TO ST. MARK

I. *The Author.*

TRADITION, from the earliest days, has ascribed this our oldest canonical Gospel to the disciple who is known in the New Testament sometimes as "John whose surname was Mark" and at other times simply as "Mark," and there is no sound reason for questioning the truth of the traditional judgment on this point. The very latest date that is assigned to the Gospel by sober criticism would bring it well within the lifetime of one who was still a young man in the year 44. We shall, then, without further discussion accept the Gospel as the authentic work of St. Mark, and proceed to consider what the New Testament has to tell us concerning the author. We are fortunately in possession of fuller information concerning him than is the case with any of the other Evangelists, with the possible exception of St. John. His mother was that Mary whose house in Jerusalem formed the central meeting-place of the primitive Christian community in that city. Dr. Sanday [1] believes that this home of Mary and her son was the very house in which the Last Supper was held. The house survived the destruction of Jerusalem and its site is still shown in our day. There is also a fixed tradition that John Mark was the young man who followed our Lord to and from the

[1] Sanday, *Sacred Sites of the Gospels,* pp 72, 73.

THE FOUR GOSPELS

Garden of Gethsemane " with the linen cloth cast about his naked body" (St. Mark xiv 51), and if this is true it would still further confirm the belief that the Last Supper was celebrated in his mother's house It would also appear that there must have existed from the beginning an intimate connection between St. Peter and the household of Mary, because it is to her house that he wends his way directly after his miraculous deliverance from the hands of Herod. The Evangelist was also closely related to another of the Apostles, St. Barnabas, whose relation he was, and it is in Barnabas' company that we find him when he begins to assume a somewhat prominent place in the sacred narrative By this time he had probably shown himself to be possessed of qualities which promised to be of substantial use in the Church, for we are told that Barnabas and Paul took him in their company when they returned to Antioch from Jerusalem on the completion of their ministry of help to that city (Acts xii 25)

Some little time later he is selected by them as their "attendant" when they proceeded on what is generally known as the "First Missionary Journey" But for some reason that is not quite clear John Mark turned his face homewards when the party reached Perga in Pamphylia, and St Paul expressed his intention of penetrating into the highlands of Asia Minor, and his defection at this point of the journey was a bitter disappointment to the Apostle Some two years or so later, when Paul and Barnabas proposed to revisit the Churches they had established on the First Journey, the latter was again desirous that Mark should accompany them, but St. Paul sternly refused to have as his companion one who "withdrew from them from Pamphylia" (Acts xv 38) This difference created a serious breach

ST MARK

between the two Apostles and led to a separation, so that eventually Barnabas and Mark sailed away unto Cyprus while Paul chose Silas as his companion for the Second Missionary Journey. It is gratifying, however, to find that St. Paul's natural indignation at Mark's desertion was not of long duration and that he soon learnt to forgive his erstwhile attendant, for we find him some years later writing to the Church of Colossæ that Mark was proposing to pay that Church a visit and requesting a cordial reception for him (Col. iv. 10). The Epistle to Philemon written at the same time as that to the Colossians from Rome shows that the Evangelist was in St Paul's company at that period, for he is mentioned in that letter by name and honoured with the title of the Apostle's "fellow-worker" (Philemon, 24) It is possible that after his departure from Rome implied in Col iv. 10 he remained in the neighbourhood of Colossæ for some years, for we find St. Paul instructing Timothy to bring Mark with him on his way from Ephesus to Rome, where the Apostle was now bravely awaiting the end (2 Tim iv 11). The tone of the Apostle's reference to Mark, now that he himself is standing on the very threshold of death, "he is useful to me for ministering," is conclusive proof that the offence of the young disciple and attendant had been long forgotten and freely forgiven, and that love unfeigned on the one side and complete loyalty on the other now reigned supreme.

To Mark's relations with St Peter there is only one explicit reference in the New Testament, viz. in 1 St. Peter v 13, where the now aged Apostle speaks of him as "Mark my son." This is, however, adequate proof of the unbroken and unceasing affection that had existed between the master and his disciple from those early days in Jerusalem when St. Peter found in the

house of Mary, the mother of Mark, a second home.
The old Apostle loved to think of the lad he had known
so well in those far-off days and of the pupil who had
sat so often and so attentively at his feet when he spoke
of the doings and sayings of the Lord Jesus. That
disciple of bygone years had now become his very son,
his companion and comfort in his old age at Rome,
where he too, like his fellow-Apostle, St. Paul, was soon
to die for his Master St. Peter's affectionate mention
of him completes what the New Testament has to say
about Mark, but tradition carries on the story and tells
us that it was he who founded the Church of Alexandria,
so renowned in later days, and that he was eventually
martyred and buried in that famous city.

Hippolytus, a Church writer of the beginning of the
third century who lived at Rome, has a story that the
Evangelist had a nickname and that he was familiarly
known as " Mark of the short finger " (κολοβοδάκτυλος)
The ordinary preface to the Vulgate also states that
after his conversion to Christianity the Evangelist
amputated one of his fingers in order to disqualify
himself for the Jewish priesthood, but the preface to
another version of the Vulgate asserts that he was born
with one short finger. The tradition that Mark did
suffer from this defect, however caused, is probably
founded on fact and it may serve to explain why John
Mark did not rise to a higher position in the Church
and why his ministry was on the whole only of a
secondary character [1]

II. *The connection between St. Peter and St. Mark's Gospel.*

(a) *The external evidence* —Far the most interesting
factor, and in some ways the most important, in refer-

[1] See Swete, *St. Mark*, pp. xxvi, xxvii

ence to this Gospel is its reputed close connection with the Apostle St. Peter. From the very first, as we have already remarked, tradition has associated our second Gospel with the great Apostle. Papias, who wrote as early as the year 150, is cited by Eusebius as saying concerning the Gospel (and be it remembered Papias is quoting an earlier authority than himself, viz. John the Presbyter) : " Mark having become the interpreter (*or* translator) of Peter wrote according to all that he (Peter) remembered (*or* mentioned), but he did not [record] in order that which was either said or done by Christ. For he neither heard the Lord nor followed Him; but afterwards, as I said, attached himself to Peter, who used to frame his teaching to meet the wants of his hearers, but not as making a connected narrative of the Lord's discourses " (Eus., *H. E.*, III. 39).

Justin Martyr, a contemporary of Papias, although he does not mention the name of St. Mark in connection with the Gospel, quotes unmistakably from it under the title of *Memoirs of Peter*

Irenæus writing about the year 180 speaks of the Gospel as follows . " After the decease of Peter and Paul, Mark the disciple and interpreter of Peter himself also handed down to us in writing the things that were preached by Peter" (*Hær* , III 1. 1)

What *Clement of Alexandria* has to contribute to this body of evidence has been already referred to in my previous lecture (see p. 8), and to this we may now add the testimony of *Tertullian*, who describes Mark as " the interpreter of Peter " (*Adv. Marcion*, IV. 2. 5).

It will have been noticed that there is a difference of opinion between what Irenæus and Clement of Alexandria have to tell us of the origin of this Gospel. Irenæus declares positively that Mark did not undertake the writing of the Gospel during the lifetime of St.

Peter, and Clement of Alexandria is equally insistent that the Apostle was alive and aware of Mark's intention to commit his oral recollections to writing. This divergence of opinion as to the exact date of the Gospel does not, however, concern us at the moment, but what is of importance is that all these ancient authorities, Papias, Justin Martyr, Irenæus, Clement of Alexandria and Tertullian, are absolutely at one in asserting that there did exist a fundamental connection between the Apostle St Peter and St. Mark's Gospel, and that the Evangelist was dependent to a substantial extent upon the Apostle for the material that he incorporated in his Gospel

(b) *Internal evidence* —The internal evidence supplied by the study of the Gospel itself confirms what we learn from tradition and tends to establish the hypothesis that behind this Gospel there stands the personality and authority of St Peter The Apostle was in our Lord's company during the whole of the period that comes under review in the Gospel, if we except the short interval that is covered by the Baptism and Temptation, both of them events which St Peter would often have heard described by Christ Himself It contains not a single word concerning the early years of Jesus or that part of His earthly life which preceded His public appearance, so that St Mark practically opens his story at the point when St. Peter attached himself to our Lord Special attention is paid to the history of the Ministry in Galilee and particularly to our Lord's activities in the neighbourhood of Capernaum, which was the Apostle's place of residence There is an expression in 11. 1, $\dot{\epsilon}\nu\ o\ddot{\iota}\kappa\wp =$ " at home " or " indoors," which seems to reproduce the very accents in which St Peter mentioned the familiar house in which he lived. A careful and fairly detailed account is given

ST. MARK

of those incidents which were witnessed by the three Apostles, St Peter, St. James, and St. John only, such as the Raising of Jairus' daughter, the Transfiguration, and the Agony in the Garden. The scene following the descent from the Mount of Transfiguration is described as it would strike one who was coming down with our Lord, who saw the excited crowd below and the distracted father rushing up the mountain to cast himself at the Master's feet.

But what, in my opinion, points most decisively to the influence of St. Peter upon the Gospel is the picture of the Apostle himself that it contains. The St. Peter of the Marcan Gospel differs substantially from the St. Peter of Apostolic tradition. It is in *St. Matthew* and not in *St. Mark* that we have incidents narrated which do honour and credit to the Apostle, such as his unique confession on the road to Cæsarea Philippi, the walking on the sea, and the finding of the piece of money in the fish's mouth. On the other hand we find St. Mark putting on record what is derogatory to the Apostle without any reserve, and it is this Gospel that is the ultimate source of much that tells against his character in the other Gospels. St. Mark tells the story of the denial in all its naked truth and lays bare before the world the Apostle's many errors and failures. It is from him too that the other Evangelists derived the incident which produced the stern rebuke, "Get thee behind me, Satan." It is difficult to believe that St. Mark, if left to his own devices, would have painted his beloved master and lifelong teacher in such sombre colours, and we are led to the conclusion that it is to the Apostle himself that we owe this element in the Gospel story. It represents the true Christian humility of St. Peter, the humility of one who remembered with sorrow how on many an occasion his conduct and attitude had been unworthy of one who had lived in such close intercourse with Jesus of Nazareth.

There are also frequent traces in the narrative of the presence of the eye-witness and of one who is describing events in which he himself took a personal part and transcribing words which he himself heard falling from the Master's lips Now this, as Papias tells us, could hardly be said of St. Mark. Among the expressions which point to the presence of the eye-witness we may quote the following: "And He *strictly* charged him and *straightway* sent him away" (i. 43), "And when He had *looked round about* on them with *anger*, being *grieved* at the hardening of their heart" (iii 5), "And he *looked round about* to see her that had done this thing" (v. 32), "And He commanded them that all should sit down by companies upon the *green grass*, and they sat down *in ranks*" (vi. 39). (The Greek expression for "in ranks" really means "like beds of flowers") The language of each one of these quotations is that of one who had studied our Lord's behaviour and attitude many a time, who had marked the precise intonation of every remark, noticed the very gesture that accompanied it, and had watched His eyes as they flashed with indignation or became bedewed with tears of affection He remembers and must tell of the impression made upon his mind by the beauty of the scene when five thousand sat down to eat on a lovely spring day and how like beds of flowers planted in the midst of the green grass the throng appeared in its multi-coloured garments The hand that transcribed the story may be that of St Mark, but the voice that speaks is unquestionably that of St. Peter who was on the spot It is he too that has kept on record the very words of the original Aramaic which our Lord used on specific occasions, *e g.* "Talitha, cumi," "Eph-

ST. MARK

phatha" and "Abba." So, then, while it is true that there is no positive statement in the Gospel itself that St. Peter was concerned in its composition, there is a great deal of indirect evidence which points in that direction and shows that the ancient tradition which looked upon the Gospel as being mainly a reproduction of the *Memoirs of Peter* is not far beside the mark.

III. *The history of the Gospel in the early Christian centuries.*

The history of the Gospel, as far as we are able to follow it, suggests that the Church in the early centuries did not place the same value upon it as was set upon the other three Gospels, for its story during these centuries is largely a record of neglect. It was all but entirely ignored by early ecclesiastical writers. This comparative neglect may be explained partly by the superior position which *St Matthew* occupied in the mind of the Church at the time and partly by the consideration that *St. Mark* was itself contained almost in its entirety in *St. Matthew* and *St. Luke*. But whatever may have been the precise reason it is an undeniable fact that not a single commentary was written on this Gospel before the fifth century, and that it was ignored and neglected to such an extent that at one time in its history there was only a single copy of it in existence, and that a battered and incomplete copy whose condition has left its mark upon every subsequent transcript that has come down to us.

This solitary copy of the Gospel broke off at the eighth verse of the sixteenth chapter with the words "For they were afraid." The last page of the only MS. that existed in the world had been torn away and lost and it has never been recovered. Two different endings were afterwards manufactured in order to compensate for the loss of the original, a longer ending, which is found in our Authorised and Revised Versions of the New Testament, and a shorter ending which is found in some MSS. and reads as follows—

" And all that had been enjoined they reported briefly to the companions of Peter. And after these things Jesus Himself from the east even to the west sent forth by them the holy and incorruptible preaching of eternal salvation "

The difference in style and language between this ending and the Gospel as a whole is patent even in an English translation. Both endings probably, and the longer one certainly, belong to the early part of the second century, because the latter seems to be referred to both by Hermas and Justin Martyr (about A.D. 150), and is definitely quoted by Irenæus as a part of St Mark's Gospel. In an age when the discovery of important literary remains is by no means an unusual incident it may not be too much to hope that the lost conclusion of St. Mark may yet be brought to light Meanwhile let us " thank the wonderful providence which preserved these priceless 'first impressions' of the life of Christ— the rugged phrases and the vivid touches of St Mark's Gospel which subsequent Evangelists softened and removed." [1]

IV. *The contents of the Gospel and its special characteristics.*

Every one of the four Gospels is written from a special standpoint, and it is this particular factor in each Gospel that explains the title attached to it in the New Testament, as, *e. g.*, " The Gospel *according to* St Matthew " or " The Gospel *according to* St. Mark." It will also be found that the purpose and special aim

[1] Armitage Robinson, *Study of the Gospels*, p. 5

ST. MARK

of each Gospel are generally defined in the verse with which the document opens. Thus St. Matthew breaks ground by tracing our Lord's human descent from David and Abraham. Christ as the Son of Promise, as He in whom all the prophecies of the Old Testament are realised, and the Heir to the throne of David is the Christ of St. Matthew, and the Messiah of the Jews as the Saviour of the world is the text of his discourse.

St Luke is the historian bent upon bestowing upon the Gentile Christian a more accurate and a more strictly historical narrative of the life of our Lord than was current before

St John opens his Gospel with the revelation of the glory of the Divine Son Christ in the fulness of His Majesty and in the ineffable glory of His Person appears on every page of the writing.

In the same manner St Mark also strikes the keynote of his message in the first verse of his Gospel with the words " The gospel of Jesus Christ, the Son of God," and what he has to tell us in the sequel is only an expansion of this theme. There are *three* main features to be noted in St. Mark's conception of Christ.

(a) *The Christ of St. Mark is the Son of God endowed with power.*—In this respect the contents of the Gospel correspond very closely with certain statements to be found in the preaching of St. Peter as it is reported in the Acts. Thus in the sermon on the Day of Pentecost St. Peter describes our Lord as " Jesus of Nazareth, a man approved by God unto you by mighty works and wonders and signs, which God did by Him in the midst of you" (Acts ii. 22), and again in his speech in the house of Cornelius the following expressions occur: " God anointed Jesus of Nazareth with the Holy Ghost and with power." " who went about doing good and healing all that were oppressed of the devil, for God was with Him" (Acts x. 38). Speaking, then, of the Christological doctrine of the Gospel it is not too much to say that it represents with marked fidelity the preaching of St Peter. The Evangelist lays special stress on the attractive power of Christ, describes how the multitudes thronged to hear Him, how they hung upon every word that fell from His lips, and how deeply they were impressed by Him. Equally emphatic is his description of our Lord's dominion over evil spirits, and there are few more significant touches in the Gospel than the way in which Satan and his hosts are represented as recognising and acknowledging the true greatness of Jesus, while the sons of men are still held in the bonds of ignorance concerning Him. So again sickness and disease in every form are pictured as doing ready and willing homage to His sovereignty, while Nature herself gives instant obedience to His commands Thus St. Mark portrays Christ as One who in every action of His life manifests His power and might.

(b) *The exceeding love of Christ.*—The strong and the tender-hearted are never so completely and so naturally blended as they are in the Christ of our second Gospel. The Mighty One in the height of His power is "moved with compassion" when the leper lies pleading for pity at His feet, His heart is full of tenderness towards the outcasts of humanity, the publicans and sinners, who crowd around Him, and He has all the love and gentleness of a mother when He so carefully provides for the physical needs of the little daughter of Jairus. Christ in the fulness of His power and yet revealing such tenderness and affection as were never seen among the children of men, this is the Christ of St. Mark's Gospel.

(c) *Jesus Christ, the Man.*—It is in this Gospel that we find the simplest and at the same time the completest outlook upon the humanity of our Blessed Lord

ST. MARK

It contains but a comparatively small amount of teaching concerning His Divinity, and speaking generally, it is only through the medium of the human that we penetrate to the Divine that is in Him. The Gospel is particularly rich in expressions which set forth the complete humanity of our Lord, and it is significant that most of these expressions are found in *St. Mark* only and not in the other Gospels. Among the traits pointing to the fulness and richness of the human nature in Christ are those which are emphasised by the Evangelist in the following citations.[1]

i 35. "He rose up and departed into a desert place and there *prayed*."

ii 27. "The sabbath was made *for man*, and not man for the sabbath"

iv 38. "And He Himself was in the stern, *asleep on the cushion*"

vi 31. "Come ye yourselves apart into a desert place *and rest a while*."

viii. 12. "And He *sighed deeply* in His spirit and saith, Why doth this generation seek a sign?"

x. 14. "But when Jesus saw it *He was moved with indignation*."

x. 21. "And Jesus looking upon him *loved him*"

The Christ of *St. Mark* then is One who feels the need of prayer, who falls asleep from weariness, is full of tender care for the welfare of His disciples, is bitterly disappointed at the conduct of the Pharisees, is full of indignation because His disciples are lacking in sympathy, and One who can love with all the intensity of the human heart. For Him also it is the need of man that is the true principle governing conduct and not the legal tradition of the Scribes.

[1] See Carpenter, *The First Three Gospels*, pp. 214 ff.

THE FOUR GOSPELS

St. Mark loves to show us the Master as a Man among men. He is careful to describe His very movements and gestures, how on one occasion He suddenly " turned Himself about," how on another " He looked round about," or how again He turned round to rebuke His followers. What a noble conception of the courage of Christ we derive from the Evangelist's description of Him striding fearlessly in front of His disciples on the way to Jerusalem to face the Cross! "And they were in the way going up to Jerusalem; and Jesus *was going before them*" (x. 32). And where in the whole range of literature, sacred or profane, can anything more eloquent or more touching be found than the verse which tells how Jesus took the little children in His arms and blessed them?

Summary.—A general view of the Gospel leaves us with the impression that the principal aim of St. Mark was to draw a simple, vivid, and correct picture of Him who brought life into the world; to let us know what manner of Man He was. His story is mainly a story of incident, and the fact that there are only four parables in the Gospel shows that the Evangelist made no real attempt to reproduce our Lord's teaching on any substantial scale. I will close the lecture by quoting almost at length a very beautiful appreciation of what is most valuable in this Gospel from the pen of Dr. Armitage Robinson.[1] " I hope that in the light of what I have said you will be encouraged to read St. Mark's Gospel with a fresh interest as the work of a single hand which paints with broad strokes and bright colours the earliest picture we possess of the Saviour of the world . . . Read it as you would read a new story which you had never heard of before; watching closely the prelude to the story, the first appearance of the young prophet

[1] *Study of the Gospels*, pp. 36-39

ST. MARK

from Nazareth, what He says and what He does, the effect produced on the people and then presently on their leaders, the bright welcome passing gradually into suspicion, the causes of the offence which He gave, the development of the political situation, and above all the unique character which little by little is unveiled to us until it reaches its climax in voluntary death. . . . You will see Jesus coming from Nazareth and promising to fulfil all expectations, offering to men good news from God. . . . He is strong to draw men after Him by a word, strong to cast out the evil spirit who interrupts His teaching, strong to heal all manner of disease, strong to resist the first outburst of popularity which threatens to divert Him from His chosen course. You will mark how this strength is linked with a tender sympathy. . . . You will see how gently He deals with those to whom His sympathetic actions give legitimate offence, how He understands and makes allowance for their natural prejudice. And at the same time you will observe how His strength and His sympathy are matched by His unwonted liberty from conventional restrictions, how really revolutionary He is, how He claims that customs are meant to serve men rather than to rule them, and how all the while He is making us look to Himself as a new fount of authority, though at first He puts forward no distinct claim to be the expected Messiah. You will specially observe that on several important occasions He speaks of Himself by a new title as 'the Son of Man' as truly human and, at the same time, representing all men. And you will find that He expects His followers to live a life like His own, a life of continuous service, seeking no private ends but perpetually giving itself to supply all human needs which cross its path, a life which finds its fitting close on Calvary, and is truly summed up in the mocking epigram hurled at Him as He hangs upon the cross, 'He saved others: Himself He cannot save.'

"So you will read, and as you read you will worship. The homage of your whole being will go out towards a life which seems both

> 'human and divine,
> The highest, holiest manhood.'

You will not understand how God and man are blended here, but you will feel that you must worship, and that it cannot be wrong to worship; for nothing so divine has been anywhere seen in nature or in human life. You will say with the amazed Roman officer who stood on guard at the foot of the cross, 'Truly this man was the Son of God.'"

LECTURE III

THE GOSPEL ACCORDING TO ST. MATTHEW

I. *The Author.*

You will remember that in our discussion concerning the author of *St. Mark* we found that there was no real difficulty in accepting the tradition that it is the authentic work of the Christian disciple of that name who is frequently mentioned in the New Testament. But when we come to deal with the first Gospel the matter is not so simple, because modern Biblical scholarship is almost unanimous in its opinion that the Gospel which bears his name was not written by St. Matthew, the Apostle. We should, however, bear in mind that, even if it could be proved beyond all question that our first Gospel is not the work of its reputed author, this would in no way militate against its authenticity as a Christian document of the Apostolic age, nor would it detract in the slightest degree from its greatness and glory as one of the most important and most precious books in the New Testament. I have already drawn your attention to the fact that the titles of our Gospels are not constituent parts of the original autographs (p. 4), and that our Gospels were in every case published without any names being attached to them. The titles were added considerably later and they only represent the general opinion of the Church at that time concerning the authorship of the several books.

Personally I am not yet convinced that the case

against the Matthæan authorship of the Gospel has been as firmly established as many scholars consider it to have been, and I believe that there is more to be said for the traditional position than they are prepared to allow. I will now place before you the arguments for and against the traditional theory as clearly and as briefly as I can, and you will then be in a position to judge whether we should still retain the old familiar idea or whether the time has arrived when we should no longer regard our first Gospel as the work of the Apostle whose name it bears

We will open the discussion by stating the case against the Matthæan authorship as it is generally presented by modern scholarship

The first point that demands an explanation from this side is, "How came a Gospel which was not written by St. Matthew to be called after his name?" And the reply to this demand would be something as follows.

St. Matthew did undoubtedly write a Gospel or something approaching a Gospel in character. Tradition in the early Christian centuries is insistent that a Gospel of St. Matthew did exist at one time, but this tradition also contains the important proviso that this Gospel of St. Matthew was written in Hebrew, which is probably only another name for Aramaic, the vernacular of the Syrian Jew at that period

This tradition concerning St. Matthew and his Gospel is found in a series of passages from the writings of early Church Fathers which have been fortunately preserved for us by the great Church historian, Eusebius, the writings themselves having in most cases perished.

The following are the writers quoted by Eusebius as sources of important information concerning St. Matthew and the Gospel that he wrote.

ST. MATTHEW 39

(a) *Papias* (about A D 150).—"Matthew wrote the 'logia' in the Hebrew dialect and each one interpreted (or translated) them as he was able" (*H. E* , iii. 39)

(b) *Irenæus* (about A D. 180).—"Matthew, then, published a writing of the Gospel, in his own tongue, i e. in Hebrew, when Peter and Paul were preaching the good news and founding the Church in Rome" (*H. E.*, v. 8 2).

(c) *Origen* (about A D. 230) —"The first Gospel was written by him who was once a publican and afterwards became an Apostle of Jesus Christ, in Hebrew, for the sake of converts from Judaism" (*H. E.*, iii 8. 2).

(d) *Eusebius* himself (A D. 260–340) also writes to the same effect. "Matthew, who had at first preached to the Hebrews, when he was about to proceed elsewhere, gave them his Gospel in their own tongue" (*H. E.*, iii 24. 6)

The historian also tells us that Pantænus is said to have gone to preach to the Indians and to have found among them a copy of the Gospel according to St. Matthew in Hebrew, which had been left by the Apostle Bartholomew (*H. E* , v 10 3)

The same tradition was current as late as the time of Jerome, who flourished during the latter half of the fourth century. We have here, then, a uniform tradition which is current as early as the middle of the second century and is repeated by writers of repute and standing in the two succeeding centuries, that our first Gospel was written by St. Matthew the Apostle in Hebrew. "But," say those who refuse to see in our canonical Gospel a genuine work of St. Matthew, the Apostle, "our *St. Matthew* was beyond question originally composed in Greek and is a compilation of materials derived from other sources, one of which sources, viz. *St. Mark*, was a Greek document whose very phraseology has been largely preserved in the first Gospel. Tradition, therefore, must have gone astray in this matter." How it went astray is thus explained. The original Hebrew Gospel of St. Matthew must have disappeared after a comparatively brief existence, although it was generally known that the Apostle had written a Gospel and what was the nature of its contents. When later a Gospel in Greek made its appearance without any particular name being attached to it and containing, among other elements, something that was strangely like the contents of the original St. Matthew, which was now completely lost, what could be more natural than to assign to the whole of the new Gospel the name of the author of a particular section of it? The Gospel must have a name, and to attach the name of St. Matthew to it was not far from the truth, and besides, it gave Apostolic authority and standing to a book which was recognised as of rare value. So the new Gospel, although written in Greek, became known as the work of St. Matthew, the Apostle, but the statement that he had written in Hebrew followed his name and became permanently associated with the Gospel.[1]

But the question naturally arises here: " Is this the only solution of the problem, and is it not possible that the explanation may lie in another direction? Even if early tradition is so insistent upon the existence of a Hebrew or Aramaic Gospel of St. Matthew, why should not our present *St. Matthew* be a translation into Greek of that original work of the Apostle?" It will be within your recollection that *St. Mark* is embodied almost in its entirety in our *St. Matthew*, and if the latter is a translation of an original Hebrew document some such procedure as the following must be conceived. *St. Mark*, which was a Greek document, must first of all have been

[1] Allen, *St Matthew*, pp lxxx, lxxxi.

ST. MATTHEW

translated into Hebrew and incorporated in that form in St. Matthew's Hebrew Gospel Then the whole of this Hebrew Gospel was translated into Greek, and the Greek of the Marcan element when so re-translated was so like that of the Greek original of *St. Mark* as to be practically indistinguishable from it. To discover a re-translation resembling the original to the extent that the Marcan element in *St. Matthew* resembles our *St. Mark* is decidedly most unusual, and most of our New Testament scholars consider that this difficulty disposes finally of the theory that our *St. Matthew* is the translation of an original Hebrew Gospel of St. Matthew, and, consequently, that our first Gospel must be the work of another hand than that of the Apostle.

To complete the case against the Matthæan authorship it is argued that a writer who was both an Apostle and an eye-witness, as St. Matthew was, would not have employed as his principal source of information the work of St Mark who was neither the one nor the other, but would have relied on his own knowledge

The case against St. Matthew's Gospel being the work of the Apostle of that name is undoubtedly strong, but there still remains something to be said for the traditional theory.

As against the argument that an Apostle and eye-witness would not have depended upon one who was neither the one nor the other as his principal source of information, we must remember that in the mind of the Apostolic Church the Gospel of St. Mark was to all intents and purposes the Gospel of St. Peter, and had behind it, therefore, Apostolic authority of first rank, and, consequently, that St. Matthew, whose place among the Twelve was a comparatively modest one, might feel that he was completely justified in using *St. Mark* as his main source of information. On the other hand, the manner in which *St. Mark* is treated by the first Evangelist, who omits, modifies, and deals with his material with the greatest freedom, seems to imply that the latter was a man of recognised position in the Church and not of merely secondary importance. An Apostle like St. Matthew would not hesitate to employ a Gospel writing which represented mainly the teaching of St. Peter, but neither would he hesitate to amend this authority in cases where his own knowledge was superior to that of the writer of that Gospel.

Again, the place occupied by St. Matthew himself in the narrative of the first Gospel gives colour to the supposition that he was the actual author. Comparing the various lists of the Apostles as they are found in the New Testament, we see that while in this Gospel the name of Matthew comes after that of Thomas, in the other lists it precedes that name. And further, it is in this Gospel only that the occupation of Matthew, that of the hated and despised publican, is mentioned.[1]

It is, however, the literary difficulty that I have sketched that is regarded as the decisive factor against the Matthæan authorship, and we must now see whether this difficulty is as insuperable as it is maintained to be.

Let us grant that the Hebrew Matthæan "logia" of Papias is identical with the document which was afterwards incorporated in our first Gospel and that it consisted mainly of the sayings and discourses of our Lord, but even so this need not preclude the possibility that the same Apostle might later have composed a Gospel in Greek, in order the more adequately to satisfy the demands of the Jewish Christians of the Dispersion among whom his labours then lay. It is well to remember that St. Matthew from the very nature of his original calling must have been familiar with the two languages

[1] Nolloth, *The Rise of the Christian Religion*, pp. 16, 17

ST. MATTHEW 43

in question, the Aramaic of the Syrian peasant and the Greek of the merchants in the Galilean towns. What was there then to prevent him from translating his Aramaic collection of the sayings of our Lord into Greek, combining these with the Greek Gospel of St. Mark, adding other material within his knowledge and so bringing into existence our first Gospel? We have seen that some scholars maintain that St. Mark first wrote his Gospel in Aramaic and that it was afterwards translated into Greek at Rome, and the same procedure may have been adopted in the case of St. Matthew's original Evangelistic document, so that the *two* main sources underlying our *St. Matthew* may have been Greek translations of documents which made their first appearance in the Aramaic tongue [1]

While, then, freely admitting that there are difficulties in ascribing our first Gospel to the Apostle St. Matthew, they are not of such a character as to compel us to abandon the traditional position without further discussion. I shall, therefore, in the remainder of the lecture speak of the Gospel as St. Matthew's, leaving the problem of the actual authorship an open question which I do not consider has yet been satisfactorily solved.

II. *St. Matthew's object in writing the Gospel.*

A very superficial study of the Gospel shows clearly that the author was a Jew writing for Jews, Christian and non-Christian, and herein lies mainly the reason why St. Matthew took upon himself to write a Gospel, when another, viz. *St Mark*, was already in existence. From the point of view of the Jewish Christian St. Mark's Gospel must have appeared eminently inadequate and unsatisfactory. There were so many questions and

[1] Nolloth, *The Rise of the Christian Religion*, p. 18.
D

problems in which the Jew, as such, was vitally interested upon which St Mark threw no light whatsoever, and his Gospel from the Jewish point of view was full of weaknesses and gaps To the Jewish Christian Christ was primarily the Messiah of Jewish prophecy and Jewish hopes, and scant justice was done in our second Gospel to this aspect of our Lord's character and mission. His Messianic claims are seldom clearly emphasised, His Davidic descent, His Birth of a Virgin, were passed over in complete silence The continuity of the New Dispensation with the Old, the conception of the Christian Church as the New Israel, the inseparable connection of the religion of Christ with the religion and history of the Jews, Christ as the realisation and fulfilment of Old Testament prophecy and as the crowning point of the revelation contained in the Jewish Scriptures,—of these and other kindred questions St Mark had little or nothing to say. Again, the Jew was keenly zealous in the matter of ethics, and all the ethical teaching of Christ contained in *St Mark* was confined to a few isolated sayings Then again the "doctrine of the last things," Christ's teaching concerning death, the end of the world, judgment, heaven, hell, and immortality, which occupied such an important place in later Jewish writings, was hardly touched upon by St Mark, and although we cannot tell precisely what the original ending of his Gospel contained, it probably did not treat the story of the Resurrection and its sequel with sufficient fulness to satisfy the demands of an inquiring Jewish mind To sum up, St Matthew discovered that among the Jewish Christians to whom he ministered as a missionary there was an urgent demand for a Gospel which would do justice to their particular point of view. " They needed information and proofs of Christ's Messiahship, of His descent from David, of His miraculous

ST. MATTHEW 45

birth, of His call to be a prophet, of His place in the long development of the chosen race; of the fulfilment of prophecies, they wanted the real principles of His moral teaching and of the teaching about the final judgment, and more evidence as to the Resurrection; of His claim, in a word, to be King of the whole world " [1]

III. *The Contents of the Gospel.*

I have already frequently called your attention to the fact that our first Gospel contains practically the whole of *St Mark* (96 per cent of its substance and about five-sixths of its actual language), and also that another Evangelistic document, now generally designated " Q," which probably corresponded to the Aramaic "logia" written by St. Matthew, has been embodied in it But St. Matthew was in possession of other resources besides *St Mark* and Q and has made a considerable use of them Included in this additional material are several important elements which are found in no other Gospel but this Perhaps the most interesting of the sections which are peculiar to *St Matthew* is that which tells of the early life of our Lord. The suggestion that the story as told in this Gospel comes from Joseph or from some one who belonged to the circle of Joseph is both reasonable and attractive It is Joseph that stands in the foreground of the picture in every incident connected with this period that is placed on record It is to him that the future of the Child to be born is revealed " For that which is conceived in her is of the Holy Ghost" (1 20) It is to him that the warning concerning the peril which threatens the Child from Herod is addressed, and it is he that receives the command to return from Egypt to Nazareth when Herod is dead and the danger has been removed. It is the story of

[1] Wilson, *The Origin and Aims of the Four Gospels*, p 43.

our Lord's childhood from the point of view of Joseph, then, that is related in this Gospel, and it is only natural to suppose that it came from Joseph himself or from one of his intimate friends.

In addition to these most interesting chapters which tell of our Lord's early life there is a group of parables which are peculiar to the first Gospel, ten in number, including the parables of the Tares, the Hid Treasure, the Pearl, the Net, the Unmerciful Servant, the Labourers in the Vineyard, the Two Sons, the Marriage of the King's Son, the Ten Virgins, and the Sheep and the Goats. All these ten parables are closely connected with each other by one line of thought running through every one of them They are all parables of "the Kingdom of Heaven," and they set forth the character of the " Kingdom " in its manifold aspects.

Only two of our Lord's miracles are recorded in this Gospel which are not found elsewhere, viz. the Healing of the Two Blind men, and the Finding of the Piece of Money in the Fish's Mouth. St Matthew was also in possession of information concerning several incidents in connection with the Passion and Resurrection which was not available, or, if available, was not utilised by the other Evangelists. He alone tells us of Judas Iscariot and the " blood money," of the dream of Pilate's wife, of the resurrection of the saints, of the sealing of the tomb, and of the bribery of the soldiers.

Reasons which determined the length of a Gospel.—It has always been a matter of discussion among scholars what were the principles which guided the Evangelists in the selection of their materials, and, particularly, why no one of them has given us anything like a complete story of the life and teaching of our Lord. It is quite clear that we get nothing more than a selection of incidents and sayings in any one Gospel and that

ST. MATTHEW 47

it is only by combining and collecting into a unity what each Evangelist has to say that we obtain a fairly general and complete outlook upon our Lord's life as a whole. Some authorities suggest that motives of space may have been at the root of the sectional and incomplete character of our Gospels, when regarded as biographies of Christ. The Gospels were written each on a separate roll of *papyrus*, and there was then a recognised convention governing the proper length of a roll. *St. Mark*, which is much the shortest of the four, would take up about 19 feet of an average roll, *St. John*, about $23\frac{1}{2}$ feet, *St. Matthew*, 30 feet, and *St. Luke*, which is the longest of the four, about 31 or 32 feet. Now the 30 feet of *St. Matthew* and the 31 or 32 feet of *St. Luke* go beyond the lengths of any well-known existing MS. A book of Homer's *Iliad* ran to a roll of about 25 feet and of the *Odyssey* to 24 feet, so that it is quite possible that St. Matthew and St Luke, at any rate, were anxious not to extend their rolls to undue lengths and, therefore, omitted material that was to be found elsewhere or substituted material that they regarded as of superior interest.[1]

IV. *How St. Matthew dealt with St. Mark's Gospel.*

It is an interesting study to observe the attitude of St. Matthew towards the work of his predecessor, St. Mark, whose Gospel he has incorporated in his own, and it is also a procedure of some importance, because the method of treatment adopted by one Evangelist towards the literary production of another throws a considerable light upon what was the general attitude of the Church in those days towards the Gospels and upon the degree of respect and reverence with which these were regarded. It is quite clear that St. Matthew

[1] See *Oxford Studies in the Synoptic Problem*, pp. 25, 26.

was not in the least animated by the feeling that the record of our Lord's life was so sacred that any tampering with its terms was in itself an act of disloyalty or sacrilege. There is in his treatment of *St Mark* not a trace of the sentiment expressed in Rev. xxii. 18, 19. " If any man shall add unto them, God shall add unto him the plagues which are written in this book · and if any man shall take away from the words of the book of this prophecy, God shall take away his part from the tree of life " St. Matthew deals with this particular source with the greatest freedom, although he is always supremely careful lest any verbal change should seriously modify the meaning or spirit of the original. If you place the canonical *St. Mark* side by side with its reproduction in St Matthew you will find that the later Evangelist has introduced changes and modifications into almost every line of his predecessor's work. And you will, moreover, discover that these alterations are not mere accidents but that a well-defined motive underlies them in practically every instance

The principal motives at the root of the changes made by St. Matthew in the text of *St. Mark* are the following.

(a) *To correct and enrich the language and style of St. Mark.*—St. Matthew was undoubtedly a much better Greek scholar than St Mark, although he does not in that respect stand in the front rank of New Testament writers. Greek culture in the New Testament reaches probably its lowest stage in our second Gospel, and we are, therefore, not surprised to find that St. Matthew, with his superior knowledge of Greek and its usages, makes frequent and fairly successful attempts to correct and improve his predecessor's style and diction. This particular type of modification can only be fully understood by a study of the Greek text of the two Gospels, and I shall, therefore, not attempt to provide you with

ST. MATTHEW 49

illustrations of St. Matthew's method in this direction, but will ask you to take it from me that quite a fair proportion of the alterations made by him in the text of *St Mark* were due to the instinct of the scholar.

(*b*) *An enhanced reverence for the Person of our Lord.*— Another motive explaining many of the most important changes made by St Matthew in his reproduction of *St Mark* is a more exalted conception of and a higher sense of reverence for the Person of our Lord. St. Mark had frequently attributed to Christ sentiments, feelings, and emotions which were perfectly natural in a mere man, but in the interval between the writing of our second and first Gospels there had been a considerable advance in the mind of the Church concerning the dignity of our Lord, so that it had come to be felt that language like that used of Him by St. Mark was no longer congruous.

St Matthew, therefore—

(1) Omits all expressions in *St Mark* which emphasise the purely human element in Christ, such as: "And when He had looked round about on them *with anger*" (St. Mark iii. 5), "And being moved *with compassion*" (i. 41), "And He *marvelled*" (vi. 6), "He was moved *with indignation*" (x. 14).

(2) He omits or modifies all expressions in *St. Mark* which seem to question our Lord's absolute power and omniscience. He omits, *e. g*, "Insomuch that Jesus *could no more openly enter* into a city" (i 45), "And He *would not* that any man should know it" (ix 30). For "And He *could do there no mighty work*" (vi. 5) he substitutes "And *He did not many mighty works* there, because of their unbelief" (St. Matt xiii. 58).

Again, St. Mark represents our Lord as asking questions, and by that very fact seems to be attributing to Him a relative ignorance. Among questions of this character found in the second Gospel are the following: "What is thy name?" (v. 9). "Who touched My garments?" (v. 30). "How many loaves have ye?" (vi. 38). "What question ye with them?" (ix. 16). "How long is it since this hath come unto him?" (ix. 21).

Now St. Matthew ignores every phrase in *St. Mark* which implies any limits to the power of Christ and every question which in any way countenances the idea that He was not omniscient.

Perhaps nothing illustrates more clearly the difference between St. Matthew's and St Mark's conceptions of what was due to the dignity of our Lord's Person than the way in which the former substitutes for "Is not this *the carpenter?*" (St Mark vi 3) his own form of the question, "Is not this the *carpenter's son?*" (St. Matt xiii 55)

(3) St. Matthew also introduces modifications into the miracle narratives of St Mark for the purpose of emphasising the immediate effect of the miracle. A frequent expression in the Gospel in this connection is "From that hour," the aim of which is to show that the power was instantaneously effective and that there was no delay between the command and the corresponding result. This tendency is plainly discernible in St. Matthew's version of the story of the cursing of the fig-tree St. Mark after recording the curse pronounced on the fig-tree simply adds, "and His disciples heard it" (xi. 14). Not till the next day (xi. 20) on their way into the city do they discover that the tree had withered. But in *St. Matthew* the tree shrivels before their very eyes and the astonished disciples ask how it happened (St. Matt. xxi. 19, 20).

Perhaps the most striking modification of the Marcan narrative in the matter of miracles found in the first Gospel is the following.

ST. MATTHEW 51

In St. Mark i. 32, 33 we read: "They brought unto Him *all* that were sick . . . and He healed *many* that were sick with divers diseases." This St. Matthew changes into: "They brought unto Him *many* possessed with devils . . . and He healed *all* that were sick" (viii. 16). St. Mark's impression of what happened was that *all* were brought into the presence of Christ and that *many* were healed, but the view of the Church had advanced by the time that St. Matthew was writing, and consequently this Evangelist tells us that *many* were brought and that *all* were healed.

(4) Finally, St. Matthew omits or modifies several questions which are attributed by St Mark to the disciples, which were not viewed by him with favour as they seemed to contain the elements of reproach and irony and, therefore, were lacking in reverence towards our Lord.

Such a question as "Master, carest Thou not that we should perish?" (St. Mark iv. 38) is changed into "Save, Lord, we perish" (St. Matt viii. 25), and another of a similar type, "Shall we go and buy two hundred pennyworth of bread?" he entirely ignores. So throughout the Gospel St Matthew either omits or modifies every phrase, expression, or question in *St. Mark* which tends in the slightest degree to detract from the Majesty and Divinity of our Lord, and the difference in tone between the two Gospels in this respect is an accurate reflection of the development of Christological conceptions in the Church during the interval that came between the writing of the one and of the other. This advance is clearly perceptible in *St. Matthew*, but it is not until we reach St. John's Gospel that we arrive at the glory and crowning point of New Testament Christological doctrine.

(c) Some of the alterations made by St. Matthew

would also seem to be due to his desire to inculcate a more favourable view of the character of the Apostles as a group. In *St. Mark* the Master is occasionally found subjecting His followers to severe rebukes, but there is hardly a trace of this element in *St. Matthew*. Take, *e g.*, the question with its implied rebuke which St. Mark places in iv. 13 in the mouth of Christ "Know ye not this parable? and how shall ye know all parables?"

In St Matt. xiii. 16–17 the rebuke is omitted, and in its place a blessing is inserted. "But blessed are your eyes, for they see and your ears, for they hear."

The question, "Why are ye fearful? have ye not yet faith?" (St Mark iv. 40) becomes in *St. Matthew* (viii. 26), "Why are ye fearful, O ye of little faith?"

St. Matthew omits the question, "Do ye not yet perceive, neither understand?" (St. Mark viii. 17), because it seems to suggest that the disciples were deficient in ordinary intelligence, and, not content with this, inserts the following statement "Then understood they how He bade them not beware of the leaven of bread, but of the teaching of the Pharisees and Sadducees" (St. Matt. xvi. 12).

St. Matthew's treatment of the Marcan story of the request of the sons of Zebedee (St. Mark x. 35–45) is both characteristic and instructive. In the corresponding passage in *St. Matthew* (xx 20–28) nothing is said of the dispute among the disciples on the way as to which of them should be the greatest, and it is the *mother* of the two disciples and *not the disciples themselves*, James and John, that proffer the request that they may sit, the one on the right hand and the other on the left in His Kingdom. It is possible, however, that we only get a complete version of the story by combining the Marcan and Matthæan narratives, and that, while the

ST MATTHEW 53

suggestion originated with the mother, the actual request was submitted by the sons, or *vice versa*.

There were also other and perhaps less important reasons why St. Matthew introduced so many changes into the work of his fellow-evangelist, such as the possession of fuller and more accurate information which enabled him to set St. Mark right on some points where the latter had gone astray.

But the ruling motives were the instinct of the scholar which led St. Matthew to correct St. Mark's style and language, an enhanced reverence for the Person of Christ, and a higher appreciation of the characters of the Apostles. In respect of the last two motives the Gospel undoubtedly reflects a corresponding development in the mind of the Church in these two directions.

V *Some characteristic features in the Gospel.*

(1) *The emphasis upon Old Testament prophecy and its fulfilment.*—Unquestionably the most striking feature in the Gospel is the pronounced emphasis which is laid throughout on Old Testament prophecy and its fulfilment in Christ Jesus. The keynote of *St. Matthew* is contained in the words, "Now all this is come to pass, that it might be fulfilled which was spoken by the Lord through the prophet" (1. 22), with which the Gospel opens, words which are frequently repeated in later chapters The Evangelist was a Jew writing for Jewish readers, and the Old Testament Scriptures naturally play a very prominent part in the Gospel. The writer reveals his object in writing in the very first verse, where he traces the descent of Jesus from David and Abraham Christ, the Messianic King and Heir of the Promise given to Abraham, is the subject of his discourse. In the mind of St. Matthew any and every incident in the historical life of Christ has already

been foreshadowed in the Old Testament, and this Gospel illustrates more clearly than any other New Testament document the truth of the old saying, "The New Testament lies hidden in the Old, the Old is revealed in the New." The Birth of Christ, His Name, the visit of the Magi, the flight into Egypt, the return to Nazareth, the preaching of the Baptist, the Ministry of Christ in Galilee, and, in truth, every incident of importance in that wonderful life had been foreseen and foretold by one prophet or another. The Evangelist is so far under the influence of this idea that he is occasionally led astray and sees correspondences where they do not actually exist. There is one instance where it looks as if St. Matthew had misunderstood the prophecy and changed the original narrative in order to adapt it to his mistaken view. In xxi. 1-8 he is evidently looking back to the words of the prophet Zechariah (ix. 9), "Behold, thy King cometh unto thee, lowly and riding upon an ass, and upon a colt, the foal of an ass," and it is clear that he is under the impression that the prophet has in mind *two* animals in this quotation, because in his narrative of our Lord's "Entry into Jerusalem" he speaks of "an ass tied and a colt with her." Now in *St. Mark*, where the original story is to be found, there is only *one* animal, the colt. St. Matthew must have forgotten for the moment what must have been quite familiar to him as a learned student of Jewish literature, viz the method in Hebrew poetry of repeating, with a kind of rhythm, in the second part of the verse or clause, what has already been stated in the first part in slightly different words. Illustrations of this peculiarity may be quoted from almost any one of the Psalms as, *e. g.*—

"At Salem is his tabernacle: and his dwelling in Sion" (lxxvi. 2); "Sing we merrily unto God our

ST. MATTHEW 55

strength : make a cheerful noise unto the God of Jacob" (lxxxi. 1).

A right understanding of Zechariah's prophecy shows that he had in view only *one* animal, but the Evangelist apparently thought that there were *two*, and modified St. Mark's story accordingly.

But although St. Matthew was a Jew, writing for Jewish readers and, consequently, interpreting Christ and His activities and attributes in the light of the Old Testament Scriptures, there is hardly a trace of the narrowness and exclusiveness of the typical Jew to be found in him. The Messiah that he proclaims was of the Jews and His mission was primarily to them, but when they rejected Him they forfeited their birthright and their privileges were transferred to the New Israel. In St. Matthew's Gospel the middle wall of partition separating the Jew from the Gentile has been demolished. Christ did not come preaching the " Kingdom of Israel " but the " Kingdom of Heaven," and it is St. Matthew that has preserved for us our Lord's world-wide commission to the Apostles, who were to make disciples of *all the nations* (xxviii 19).

(2) *The Gospel of the Kingdom.*—The most familiar phrase in the Gospel, where it occurs thirty-two times, is " The Kingdom of Heaven." The conception, but not the name, is borrowed from the Old Testament and pre-Christian Jewish literature, in which it occupies a prominent place as a constituent element of what is now generally termed Jewish Eschatology, or " the Doctrine of the Last Things." In this later Jewish literature the term contemplated the coming of the age when the absolute sovereignty of God would be universally acknowledged, an age to be ushered in by the dawn of the Messianic Kingdom, when the Son of Man would appear in the clouds of Heaven at the end

of the world to reign with His saints for ever, and, speaking generally, this is the sense in which the term is used in St Matthew's Gospel. Christ proclaimed the near advent of the Kingdom and His disciples were to proclaim it too and to pray for its coming It would not come within the lifetime of Christ, but after His death and yet within the lifetime of that generation. In that Kingdom the Apostles would sit on twelve thrones judging the twelve tribes of Israel. Its subjects were to be those who were "pure in heart," "persecuted for righteousness' sake," those "whose righteousness shall exceed the righteousness of the scribes and Pharisees," and whose character was like that of little children It is in this eschatological sense that the term is used in the majority of the parables, and especially in that group of parables which we have noted as being peculiar to this Gospel The question whether the "Kingdom of Heaven" in our Lord's teaching had any other meaning beyond the eschatological has been a matter of wide discussion among scholars in recent years. Now even if it be granted that our Lord Himself only used the term in that limited sense there is little room to doubt that St Matthew saw in it more than a mere eschatological reference There are frequent hints in the Gospel that in the mind of the Evangelist the "Kingdom" was a present reality, or, to be more precise, that this life as a period of preparation for the coming of the "Kingdom" becomes for him so blended with the "Kingdom" itself that it is difficult sometimes to distinguish the one from the other. In this sense, then, the "Kingdom" is an entity whose blessings are within reach of men in the present life and is, therefore, practically identical with the Church on earth We shall, therefore, not be far beside the mark if we designate *St. Matthew* as not only the "Gospel

ST. MATTHEW 57

of the Kingdom " but also as the " Gospel of the Church." We should note that he alone of the four Evangelists introduces the word "church" (ἐκκλησία) into his Gospel, and it is he that has most to tell us concerning the Church as a fundamental Christian institution. According to St. Matthew Christ Himself constituted the disciples into a Church, ordained that admission into it should be through Baptism in the name of the Holy Trinity, appointed a ministry for it in the persons of the Apostles, who were to rule and to have power to loose and bind, and to whom were entrusted the functions of preaching and baptising St Matthew also tells us how careful the Master was to provide for the public worship of the Church in His promise that where two or three were gathered together in His name there would He also be in the midst, how He taught His disciples to pray, and how He instituted the two great Sacraments of the Church The practical Christian life is outlined with considerable detail, its duties, prayer, fasting, and almsgiving, and its virtues, humility, mercy, love, self-denial, and faith, being duly emphasised In short, the Gospel is permeated through and through by the ecclesiastical atmosphere and spirit

(3) *The Gospel of Christian Ethics* —I have already referred to the fact that *St Mark* contains only a very small fraction of our Lord's teaching, and that one of the reasons which moved St Matthew to write his Gospel was his sense of the inadequacy of his predecessor's work in this particular direction Until our first Gospel was published the Christian of the Apostolic age had to depend on tradition for his knowledge of what life in Christ demanded of him in the matter of character and conduct It was not until St Matthew had gathered together all that he remembered of our Lord's teaching on its ethical side and had formed out of these scattered

recollections what we have learnt to call "the Sermon on the Mount," that the Church came into possession in a permanent form of what is nothing less than a remarkably full exposition of the practical life of the Christian Perhaps the greatest debt, therefore, that the present world owes to St. Matthew is the existence of this written unquestioned standard of Christian life to appeal to, with its never-failing inspiration and its many other qualities that constitute it a treasure of priceless value.[1]

[1] Wilson, *The Origin and Aims of the Four Gospels*, pp. 54-56.

LECTURE IV

THE GOSPEL ACCORDING TO ST LUKE

I. *The Author.*

ONE of the most satisfactory and gratifying results of recent New Testament criticism is the substantial advance that has been made in the direction of proving that our third Gospel is the authentic work of St. Luke. Harnack, who was at one time strongly opposed to the Lucan authorship of the Gospel, has now become a convert to the traditional theory and has devoted much time and labour to bringing others to the same way of thinking He has also received able support from scholars in this country, and the names of Ramsay and Hawkins will always be remembered with gratitude by those who love to think that our third Gospel comes from the hands of the "beloved physician" There is not the slightest hint of a direct character in the Gospel itself pointing to the identity of the writer, but the author of the third Gospel has also another book to his credit in the New Testament, and it is in this second book, viz. the *Acts of the Apostles,* that the clue is found which enables us to put our hands on the writer of both these documents There are substantial sections of the *Acts* in which the author designates the company whose activities he is concerned with by the personal pronoun "*we*," thus implying that he himself was a member of the company on the particular occasions in question. And further, the elaborate linguistic comparison between the "*we*" sections and the rest of the *Acts* instituted by Hawkins and adopted and completed by Harnack seems to establish the conclusion that the author of the journal was also responsible for the composition of the whole book. Consequently if we can lay our hands on the author of the "*we*" sections we have discovered who wrote the *Acts* and also, what is our special concern at the moment, who was the author of the third Gospel.

Now taking the personal pronoun "*we*" as it occurs in the *Acts* as our guide we acquire the following particulars with reference to the personality and activities of the writer of this journal If we follow the accepted text of the Acts the "*we*" sections open at xvi. 10, but in what is called the "Western Text" there is inserted in xi. 27 the phrase "*we* being gathered together," which many important authorities are inclined to regard as an original part of the verse If this be true the author of the "*we*" sections was in St Paul's company at Antioch before he and Barnabas paid the visit to Jerusalem in connection with the relief fund, *i. e* somewhere about the year 44. But if we pin our faith to the usual text the author makes his first appearance on the scene at Troas during the second Missionary Journey in the autumn of 48.

Ramsay makes the interesting suggestion that he was "the man from Macedonia" who appeared in a vision to St. Paul at Troas and induced the Apostle to cross the Ægean and to undertake the mission to Europe which had such momentous results Whether Ramsay is correct or not in his suggestion it is quite certain that the writer in question was with St. Paul at Troas at the time of the vision, that he accompanied him on the voyage to Macedonia, and that he was a member of the band of missionaries who came to Philippi (xvi. 11–13).

ST. LUKE 61

He seems to have remained in that city when the Apostle departed for Thessalonica, for the "*we*" disappears from the narrative for several chapters and does not emerge again until St. Paul pays his second visit to Philippi (xx. 6), where the writer had probably spent the whole of the interval between the Apostle's two visits. From this point onwards the "*we*" is used consistently to the end of the *Acts*, showing that the author was in St Paul's company practically without a break during the period covered by the last nine chapters of the book. He journeyed with him from Philippi to Jerusalem and was an eye-witness of the important incidents which befell him in that city, the arrest, the speech on the Castle stairs, and his defence before the Jewish Council. He accompanied the Apostle when he was transferred to Cæsarea and remained in his neighbourhood during some portions, if not during the whole, of the two years' imprisonment in Cæsarea, and was certainly among the audience when St. Paul delivered his famous defence before Agrippa and Festus. Finally he accompanied the Apostle on that historic voyage to Rome, and it is to his skilled hand that we are indebted for that vivid and descriptive narrative of the storm in the Adriatic, the shipwreck and landing in Malta, and the arrival in the Imperial city. The closing verses of the *Acts* also imply that he remained in Rome for some time after the Apostle had taken possession of " his own hired house."

And now the question arises, "Who was this companion of St. Paul who wrote the journal of the Apostle's journeys and activities ? " because, as we have already seen, the writer of the journal was almost unquestionably the author of our third Gospel. Now we know that St. Luke was a prominent member of St. Paul's immediate circle of companions and also that he was with the Apostle at certain definite moments of the period covered by the "*we*" sections. We know, *e g*, that he was with the Apostle at Rome during the first imprisonment, because his name appears in two of St. Paul's Epistles written at that particular time, viz. in Col. iv. 14 and Philemon 24, among those who were in the Apostle's near neighbourhood But there were others also who were in very close association with St. Paul during the period in question, such as Timothy, Titus, and Silas, any one of whom might have written the journal incorporated in the *Acts*. Tradition has, however, from the earliest days attributed the authorship of the Gospel and the *Acts* to St. Luke, and as he fits the situation in the *Acts* as well as any of his companions there is no sound reason for questioning the truth of a very early and consistent tradition or for looking for the author in any other direction than that of St Luke. The theory that both the Gospel and the *Acts* are the work of "the beloved physician" is also confirmed by the number of technical medical terms that are found in both documents, which seem to imply a considerable knowledge of the art of medicine on the part of the author.

The following summary represents the results of our inquiry. A scientific analysis of the linguistic phenomena of the "*we*" sections of the *Acts* and of the *Acts* as a whole establishes the fact that the author of the sections was also responsible for the whole book. Further, the author of the Gospel being unquestionably identical with the author of the *Acts* is, therefore, the author of the journal incorporated in the latter book, who is St. Luke, "the beloved physician," and the intimate friend and companion of St. Paul.

With the exception of the information conveyed in this journal and in the scanty references to him in the Pauline Epistles we know very little concerning St Luke.

ST. LUKE 63

It is quite manifest from his writings that he was a Gentile and not a Jew, and his style and diction prove that he was a man of education and culture, such as we might look for in a member of a learned profession. Tradition affirms that he was a native of Antioch in Syria, and if the Western reading of Acts xi. 27, to which I have already referred, is correct it tends to confirm this tradition. Sir W. Ramsay, as you will remember, identifies St. Luke with "the man of Macedonia," and he in turn is supported by the generally accepted text which represents the Evangelist as having first come into touch with St. Paul at Troas, just before the mission into Macedonia was embarked on It is quite a reasonable suggestion that what originated the intimacy between St Luke and the Apostle were the latter's frequent illnesses which called for the constant attendance of a medical man. But this alone would not account for the very close and affectionate connection that existed between the two In two out of the three passages in his letters where St Paul mentions the name of Luke there is in the very tone of the references themselves, "Luke the beloved physician," "Only Luke is with me," a revelation of the deepest personal love on the Apostle's part, and, on the other hand, every line of St. Paul's story as related by St Luke reveals how whole-heartedly that love was returned. It was not merely the Apostle's weakness, therefore, that constituted the bond between them. Stronger than the mere sense of the Apostle's need of his services was the attraction exercised on St Luke by the unique personality of St. Paul and by the power of the religion he preached and practised, an attraction which reacted on a nature which was unusually capable of steadfast loyalty and devoted service. In a word, it is the religion of Jesus Christ producing a beautiful fellowship between two great souls that alone accounts for the affectionate relationship that existed between the Apostle and his faithful physician and companion.

The New Testament contains all the information that we possess concerning St. Luke that is of any real historical value There is, it is true, a comparatively early tradition that after St. Paul's death he preached in Dalmatia, Macedonia, and Gallia (which probably means Galatia), and that he crowned a life of unceasing service to the Church by dying a martyr's death, his bones being afterwards removed to Constantinople, but it is difficult to attach much weight to these statements There is one legend, however, concerning St. Luke which, quite apart from the question of its historical worth, is very attractive and instructive as well A tradition, which dates from the sixth century and may be even older than that, tells us that St. Luke was a painter. The old story describes how Eudoxia, the Empress from Constantinople, discovered in Jerusalem a portrait of the Blessed Virgin reputed to be the work of the Evangelist, and how she sent the picture to the Byzantine capital as a present for her daughter Pulcheria, the consort of the reigning Emperor Theodosius. The picture was brought to Venice in the thirteenth century, and a portrait of the Virgin supposed to have been the work of St. Luke is to be seen to-day in the church of S. Maria Maggiore in Rome.

There is probably little if any historical truth in the legend, but it serves a useful purpose as illustrating the impression made by St. Luke and his writings on the mind of the Church in very early days, how from the beginning of Christian history his name came to be closely associated with Christian art The earliest specimens of Christian mural drawings are to be found in the Catacombs in Rome, and among the examples

ST. LUKE

that still survive the most common and probably the most ancient is the representation of Christ as the Good Shepherd rescuing the Lost Sheep, as described by St Luke in the familiar parable. The great majority of the sacred subjects that were depicted on the walls of our ancient churches were also selected from St. Luke's Gospel, such as the Annunciation, the Shepherds of Bethlehem, the Manger, Christ among the Doctors, and parables like those of the Good Samaritan and the Prodigal Son The legend in question as far as it speaks of the influence of St. Luke upon Christian art is, therefore, true in idea if not in actual fact. And further, if St. Luke was not an artist in the stricter sense of the term, an artist he certainly was, because the whole realm of literary art presents no nobler or more arresting pictures than those painted in words by St. Luke in his incomparable Gospel.

II. *St. Luke's purpose in writing the Gospel*

St. Luke differs from all his fellow-evangelists in that in the very first verse of his Gospel he clearly defines the reason why he is adding another to the list of existing Gospels His book is dedicated to a person called Theophilus for the purpose of confirming his trust and confidence in the faith that he has adopted It is not easy to decide whether Theophilus was an actual disciple or a mere name symbolising a particular class of persons, viz. those who " loved God," for the name means, " the friend of God." The probability is that he was an actual historical personage, because St Luke addresses him as " most excellent Theophilus," a title which was generally associated with a person holding high official rank. But whether Theophilus stands for an actual individual or is a merely symbolical name, it is quite evident that he is meant to represent the typical Gentile Christian who was yearning for more light upon Christ and His teaching than was available in the sermons, addresses, and Christian writings that were already within his reach. The following features in the Gospel show that it was mainly the Gentile Christian that the Evangelist had in view. He employs Greek names where the other Evangelists have the Hebrew equivalents, he dates the incidents in his narrative in accordance with the prevailing secular custom by the year of the reign of the ruling Emperor, he traces the descent of Jesus from Adam, the father of all men Comparatively little attention is bestowed upon the prophecies of the Old Testament, and all through the Gospel he is explaining Jewish practices and customs, a perfectly superfluous proceeding if his readers had been Jews to whom such practices were so familiar. St. Luke was, then, a Gentile, and judging from his literary and other qualities a Greek (Ramsay points to his love of the sea as eminently characteristic of the Greek), writing for his brethren, the Gentile Christians. He had two practical objects in view in undertaking this task, viz. to put forth a Gospel that was comparatively complete, and secondly a Gospel that was historical. Both these aims are set forth in the prologue to the Gospel. He declares that he "had traced the course of all things ... *from the first*" (1 3), which constitutes his claim to the comparative completeness of his work, and in 1. 4 he adds that he had traced the course of all things *accurately* in order that Theophilus "might know the *certainty* concerning the things wherein he was instructed," claiming again that what he writes is the historical truth concerning Christ and His religion.

What St Luke meant by a complete Gospel is revealed to us by a glance at his own production. The story must start from the very beginning, and the beginning

ST. LUKE 67

is not the birth of Christ, but the promise of the coming of the Forerunner, John the Baptist. And we mark the same factor at the other end of the story. He does not merely relate the narrative of the Resurrection and of the post-resurrection appearances of our Lord like the other Evangelists, but carries on the tale to its logical conclusion and completes his work with the story of the Ascension into Heaven. He has also collected a quantity of information concerning Christ and His ministry which is not available in any other Gospel, and it is noteworthy that among this special material gleaned by St. Luke are to be found some of the most precious treasures in Christian literature. The Evangelist's keen desire to include in his Gospel all that was worth preserving is very manifest and the Gospel throughout betrays the hand of a historian of high rank.

III. *The sources of the Gospel*

St. Luke in his prologue to the Gospel (1. 1–4) makes note of the fact that others before him had taken in hand the writing of gospels, and goes on to explain, as I have already remarked, that his principal aim is to put forth a narrative of our Lord's life and work that shall improve upon its predecessors in the matters of chronological order, historical accuracy, and completeness. That he might the better accomplish this purpose he has consulted the best authorities available, viz. those persons "which from the beginning were eyewitnesses and ministers of the word" (1. 2). You will remember how in our first lecture (pp. 11–13) when we were discussing the character of the sources upon which the Synoptic Gospels were based, we came to the conclusion that in the main they were written sources, and, on St. Luke's own showing, this would seem to be particularly true of his Gospel. It will also be within your recollection that St. Luke, like his fellow-evangelist St Matthew, has incorporated *St. Mark* (about four-fifths of the substance of the second Gospel is to be found in the third) and the document called Q in his own work As a considerable amount of time has been devoted to the discussion of these two sources, all that I propose to do here is to show how St. Luke dealt with them when he embodied them in his Gospel

(a) *St. Luke's use of St. Mark* —St. Luke in his use of St Mark's Gospel has worked much on the same lines as St. Matthew did under similar circumstances. He also has subjected the second Gospel to frequent and substantial changes, and these alterations are often based on reasons similar to those which influenced St. Matthew. St Luke is second to none of the New Testament writers as a Greek scholar, and in this respect is far ahead of St Matthew, so that we are not surprised to find that he is frequently dissatisfied with the poor style and diction of St Mark, and that a great proportion of the modifications that he introduces into his predecessor's work are due to his superior knowledge of Greek. He also is imbued with a much higher conception of the Person of our Lord Jesus Christ than was current in *St Mark*, and has given clear expression to this enhanced Christological outlook in the method with which he deals with some of his fellow-evangelist's somewhat crude and rugged language and ideas. But St. Luke is more inclined than the first Evangelist to omit or curtail St. Mark's stories, being probably influenced in this matter by the profusion of other material that he had at his disposal and considered to be of greater value and more deserving of a place in his Gospel than what was contained in *St. Mark*. We find, *e. g.*, that he has entirely omitted one complete section of

ST. LUKE

St. Mark, viz vi 45–viii 26, and that he has cut short many other passages. The omission of St. Mark vi 45–viii 26 is somewhat difficult to understand, because it contains material that might be expected to make a special appeal to him as a Gentile Christian In this section St. Mark tells the story of the journey of our Lord and the Twelve into the heathen and Gentile districts of Tyre, Sidon, and Decapolis, including the incidents of the healing of the daughter of the Syro-Phœnician and the feeding of four thousand Gentiles. This is apparently the only occasion on which our Lord departed from His rule of confining His ministrations within the Jewish borders and paid a visit of mercy to Gentile districts, thus faintly foreshadowing His world-wide mission, and yet St. Luke, with his consuming interest in Gentile Christianity and its history, completely ignores the visit. Some scholars suggest that the omission was accidental In St Mark vi. 42–44 the subject of the feeding of the multitudes is mentioned and the same subject crops up again in viii 19–21, and it is possible that when St. Luke, who had left off copying St Mark at vi. 44, came to resume his work his eye was caught as he was unfolding the roll by the similar lines in viii. 19–21, and that he, therefore, continued his copy at the wrong point and so left out a whole section of the second Gospel. When we remember what a cumbrous article a roll of the Gospel was to handle a mistake of this character becomes quite intelligible. Others again are of opinion that the omission of the section by St Luke was deliberate and intentional, because, although it contained material which in some respects was in accord with his special interests, yet, from another point of view, it was not quite satisfactory. It is quite clear that St. Matthew and St. Mark both regarded our Lord's journey over the border as being of an exceptional character. St. Mark speaks of it as being for the purpose of retirement only (vii. 24), and both Evangelists look upon the healing of the Syro-Phœnician's daughter as an unpremeditated act of mercy on our Lord's part. It is quite possible, therefore, that St. Luke felt that the reproduction of the narrative might repel rather than attract his Gentile readers, and would not tend to foster good relations between Jews and Gentiles in the Christian Church, and, consequently, omitted it from his Gospel.

(b) *St. Luke's use of Q.*—There is a substantial difference between St. Luke's treatment of Q and the way in which this document is dealt with by St. Matthew, and more especially in the matter of the Sermon on the Mount. In *St Matthew* the sermon takes the form of a single connected discourse, delivered from beginning to end on one definite occasion, but in *St. Luke* passages from this presumably connected discourse are scattered freely over the whole Gospel, and without any apparent connection between one passage and another. Which of the two Evangelists, then, has adhered to the original form of Q ? It is natural for us to suppose that the Sermon on the Mount was, like any other sermon, delivered continuously on some particular occasion and that St. Matthew has reproduced it in its original character, but a careful study of this Evangelist's method of building his Gospel rather tends to prove that in this particular aspect of Q St. Luke has kept closer to the primitive document. There is a definite principle governing St. Matthew's arrangement of the materials he borrowed from Q, which consists in collecting into a group passages which deal with a particular subject. St. Luke, on the other hand, seems to have been led by his historical instinct to place the sayings in connection with the actual occasions on which they were uttered. It is

ST. LUKE

probable, therefore, that his arrangement is more true to fact than that of St. Matthew and that the Sermon on the Mount in the form in which it is found in our first Gospel represents a collection of addresses delivered at various times rather than a single continuous discourse. It is difficult to discover any sound reason why St. Luke should split a single long discourse into a series of short passages and scatter them throughout his Gospel, whereas, with our knowledge of St. Matthew's special method, it is easy to understand why he joined together a number of isolated addresses and fused them into one.

(c) *Material peculiar to St. Luke.*—The most interesting elements in St. Luke are not those the Evangelist borrowed from St. Mark or Q, but those which are peculiar to himself and are not forthcoming in any other Gospel. As a matter of fact what gives *St. Luke* its unique character and converts it into a Christian document of priceless value is what this Evangelist, and no one else, tells us about our Lord and His teaching.

There are three sections peculiar to this Gospel which call for special attention.

(1) *The first two chapters of the Gospel.*— In the opening chapters St. Luke is manifestly working on a source which has not been utilised by any other Evangelist. We are indebted to him for all we know about the early history of the Baptist, for that incomparable setting of the story of our Lord's infancy with its pictures of the Annunciation, the Manger, the Shepherds, the Presentation in the Temple, and for the one incident in His boyhood that is related in the Gospels, the visit to Jerusalem when He was twelve years old. St. Luke is also the hymnologist of the early Christian Church, and without his Gospel we should have been deprived

of the beautiful Canticles, the Benedictus, Magnificat, and Nunc Dimittis, which for so many centuries have had an honoured place in the public services of the Church. In my previous lecture, as you will remember, it was suggested that it was Joseph or some one belonging to his circle that was primarily responsible for the narrative of the birth and infancy of our Lord as it is given in *St Matthew*, and it is equally reasonable to see in the version of the story that is presented by St. Luke the hand of the Virgin Mother or of one of her intimate associates. St. Luke's narrative is essentially the story of the Divine Son as told by the Blessed Mother, and it is her voice and emotions that give character to the tale.

(2) *The Travel Document* (chaps. ix 51–xviii. 14) — There is also another section, comprising more than a third of the Gospel and including chaps. ix. 51–xviii. 14, to which there is practically nothing to correspond in any of the other Gospels. This section, sometimes called the "Travel Document," contains the record of our Lord's last journey to Jerusalem If we possessed only *St. Matthew* and *St. Mark* we might suppose that the journey from Galilee to Jerusalem for the last Passover occupied only a week or two, but St. Luke's narrative enables us to see that it must have covered several months. In the course of that journey our Lord travelled first eastwards along the southern part of Galilee and then southwards through Peræa, but always with Jerusalem in view as His true destination. Embedded in this "Travel Document" lie the most attractive and inspiring of our Lord's parables, such as those of the Good Samaritan and the Prodigal Son. It has been noticed that a strong womanly element runs through the document and that it manifests on the part of its ultimate author a considerable degree of sympathy

ST. LUKE 73

with the Samaritans and some familiarity with Herod and his court. We are, therefore, not surprised to find that it is widely suggested that a woman's hand was concerned in the source underlying St. Luke's version of this document. Some attribute this womanly element to the daughters of Philip the Evangelist, and quote in support of their suggestion a statement from Eusebius that "the four daughters of Philip transmitted stories of the old days" We know that Philip and his daughters were resident at Cæsarea and we know further that St. Luke spent some considerable time in that city when St. Paul was imprisoned there. During that period the Evangelist must have been brought into frequent contact with the household of one who held a leading position among the Christians of Cæsarea, and it is quite a plausible suggestion that he may have learnt much from Philip and his daughters concerning the particular period in our Lord's ministry that we are discussing. Philip was naturally interested in, and in sympathy with, the Samaritans, because they were the firstfruits of his missionary preaching, and his daughters were there to see that justice was done in the story to the women who were our Lord's devoted companions, as well as to what our Lord Himself had to say concerning women in general. It is to the household of Philip at Cæsarea, then, that some scholars would have us look for both the womanly and the Samaritan elements in the "Travel Document." Personally I prefer another theory which finds St. Luke's informant among the very women who were in our Lord's company on the way to Jerusalem and were eye-witnesses of all that happened there. Three of these women are mentioned by name, Mary Magdalene, Susanna, and Joanna, the wife of Chusa Of the three Joanna would seem to fit the situation best. St. Luke is evidently interested in her because he is the only Evangelist to mention her by name, and it may be that this interest in her is a token of the gratitude he felt towards Joanna because of the service she rendered in providing him with the information contained in the narrative of this fateful journey. Further, she was a woman, the wife of an official at Herod's court, and was familiar with the Samaritans and their ways, and, therefore, satisfies all the conditions of the problem admirably

(3) *St. Luke's story of the Passion.*—A third section of the Gospel in which St Luke seems to be following a line of his own is that which contains the narrative of the Passion. Here his story is incomparably fuller and richer than the Passion stories of the other Evangelists. One great Lucan scholar (Sir John Hawkins) has suggested that at one time St. Luke was a preacher of the gospel like St Paul, and that the Apostle was thinking of this particular side of his companion's activities when he referred to him as "Luke, my fellow-worker" in Philemon 24. Hawkins would see, then, in St. Luke's version of the Passion story a reproduction of the oral gospel preached and proclaimed by him in his capacity as a Christian missionary. In concentrating attention upon the Cross and the Resurrection St Luke would only be following in the footsteps of the Apostle himself, who, in contrast with the Gospel record as a whole, confined his preaching, as far as it consisted in setting forth facts, almost entirely to the Death and Resurrection of our Lord. It is possible, therefore, that the particular form which St. Luke's story of the Passion takes may be due to the influence of St. Paul upon the Evangelist's preaching, and that this section of the Gospel, so rich and so full in its narrative of that eventful period, is practically a reproduction of the Pauline Gospel as it was proclaimed throughout the world. Whether we

ST. LUKE 75

accept this suggestion or not, it is tolerably certain that it was from St. Paul that St. Luke learnt the true significance of the Cross of Christ.

IV *Some characteristic features of the Gospel.*

The following are some of the most striking features of the third Gospel.

(1) *Its catholicity.*—It is only natural to find in a Gospel addressed to the Gentile Christian Church a broad outlook and a catholic sympathy, and we are, therefore, not surprised that St. Luke teaches more clearly than any of the other Synoptists that Christ is *the Saviour of the world.* We meet in this Gospel with that realisation of the true catholicity of the religion of Christ which was so characteristic of St. Luke's master and teacher, St. Paul, who proclaimed that "there can be neither Jew nor Greek, there can be neither bond nor free, there can be no male and female: for ye are all one *man* in Christ Jesus" (Gal iii. 28). The barrier separating the Jew from the Gentile has in this Gospel been destroyed to its very foundations, and if there is any bias displayed in favour of the one side or the other it is no longer the Jew but the Gentile that is in the position of privilege. In the description of Christ's mission to the world in the "Song of Simeon," "the light to lighten the Gentiles" takes precedence of "the glory of His people Israel." The descent of Jesus is traced from Adam, the father of all men, and not from Abraham, the founder of the chosen race. Strangers like Naaman, the Syrian, and the Widow of Sareptah are mentioned in tones which breathe the sincerest respect for what was best in the old heathen world. It is the one Gospel that seeks to do justice to the Samaritan, so despised by the typical Jew, and it is St. Luke alone that has preserved for us the expression of our Lord's

F

high appreciation of what was estimable in that race by relating the story of the Ten Lepers and the parable of the Good Samaritan. Two noble ideas shine through every page of the Gospel, the universal love of the Father, and the mission of the Divine Son to redeem all mankind

(2) *The Gospel of the Individual* —Side by side with St. Luke's proclamation of the universality of the redemptive love of Christ stands his emphasis upon the message of our Lord to the individual. The Evangelist's conception of the individualistic and personal nature of our Lord's teaching comes out most clearly when we compare the parables recorded by St. Luke with those incorporated in the first Gospel. The parables which give a special character to *St. Matthew* are in every instance parables of the "Kingdom" and are mainly intended to illustrate the growth and consummation of the Kingdom of God. St Luke has included twenty-three parables in his Gospel, and of these eighteen are peculiar to himself. These, in contrast to St. Matthew's parables, are all stories of men and women and common things and contain the message of salvation to the individual. "They teach us that we men, however lost, are still individually loved by our Heavenly Father and sought for, are longed for and welcomed back, that souls darkened by sin and estranged from God may be restored by God's grace, they teach the universality of God's love; that it goes out into the highways and hedges. It is in St. Luke we read of the value of the Publican's confession, of the bliss of Lazarus "[1] The principle of God's relation to the individual which in the Old Testament is hardly perceptible until we reach the period of the great prophets, Jeremiah and Ezekiel,

[1] Wilson, *The Origin and Aims of the Four Gospels*, p. 67.

ST. LUKE 77

has come to its own in St. Luke's Gospel and remains one of its greatest treasures.

(3) *The Gospel of Forgiveness.*—Correlative with St. Luke's conception of our Lord's teaching as a message to the individual soul is his insistence upon the gospel of Christ as being essentially the proclamation of God's forgiveness to the sinner A mere glance at the passages which are only found in this Gospel shows how vital to the Evangelist was this aspect of our Lord's preaching and example. It is St. Luke only who tells the story of the woman who was a sinner who washed the feet of Jesus with her tears and loved much because she was forgiven much.

The parables which he alone relates are also permeated with the thought of forgiveness as, *e g.*, the parables of the Two Debtors, the Pharisee and the Publican, and, above all, the parable of the Prodigal Son. It is significant that only in this Gospel do we find mention of our Lord's beautiful prayer on the Cross, "Father, forgive them, for they know not what they do." The Christ of *St Luke* is ever proclaiming the forgiveness of God to the penitent sinner, the vital need of the spirit of forgiveness among men. He is the Christ who crowns His teaching by His own prayer on the Cross that the Father might forgive those who were using Him so despitefully.

(4) *The Woman's Gospel.*—There is no feature that is more characteristic of our Gospel than the honourable position which is accorded in it to woman as such No writer in the New Testament has been so careful to preserve for posterity that particular aspect of the teaching of Christ which has been the strongest influence in uplifting the woman from the position of comparative contempt and dishonour which was hers in the world generally before the dawn of Christianity The Evan-

gelist's attitude in this matter was probably due in some degree to the fact that he was a Greek and not a Jew, for the Greek was imbued with a much higher conception of the rightful position of the woman both in public and private life than was possessed by the Jew. History teaches us that women were regarded with greater honour and respect in Greece than in any other part of the world, and a study of St. Luke's writings shows how loyal he remained to the traditions of his race on this point. Lydia and Priscilla as individuals, and the women of Macedonia as a class, receive their due meed of attention in the *Acts*, and in the Gospel Christ as the Saviour of the woman is one of the dominant notes. The Evangelist's reverence for women is manifested at the very opening of the Gospel. If you compare the stories of our Lord's infancy in the first and third Gospels you will immediately realise the difference between St. Matthew, the Jew, and St. Luke, the Greek in their outlook upon women. In *St. Matthew* it is Joseph who in every emergency takes the lead, but in St. Luke's picture of the same period the Blessed Virgin stands in the foreground. And what is true of the earlier chapters obtains all through the Gospel. Anna stands by Simeon's side when he welcomes the Holy Child in the Temple, and it is in this Gospel only that we read of the Widow of Nain and of the devoted ministrations of Mary and Martha to the Saviour. It is St. Luke only that tells us the names of the women who accompanied our Lord on His travels and shared with Him all they possessed, and he alone relates the parables of the Widow and the Unjust Judge, and the Woman with the Lost Piece of Money. It is the same Evangelist who describes that scene, so full of pathos, where our Lord bears His Cross on the way to Calvary and the women of Jerusalem

ST. LUKE 79

weep in deepest sympathy with Him. What the women of the Christian world owe to St. Luke is immeasurable, because he stands alone among the writers of the New Testament in his conception of the services rendered by woman to Christ and to His Kingdom and of her true place in that Kingdom.

(5) *The Gospel of the Poor.*—Our knowledge of what our Lord had to say on the subject of wealth is practically confined to what we learn from St. Luke. A comparison of his version of the first Beatitude with St. Matthew's will at once enable you to recognise our third Evangelist's special interest in the poor as such. Where St. Matthew reads, " Blessed are the poor in spirit, for theirs is the Kingdom of Heaven," St. Luke has " Blessed are *ye poor :* for *yours* is the Kingdom of Heaven." For him poverty in the ordinary sense of the term and not merely " poverty in spirit" constitutes a qualification for the Kingdom of God Our Lord's teaching concerning the temptations and the spiritual dangers associated with the possession of riches is brought out time after time. Those sections of the Gospel to which the other Synoptists provide no parallels speak eloquently of the importance attached by St. Luke to the Master's message of comfort to the poor. Our Lord's sermon at Nazareth (iv. 17–21) with its key-note " to preach good tidings to the poor," which is recorded by St. Luke only, is a case in point. So again the Magnificat, the Song of the Blessed Virgin, breathes throughout the same spirit. " He hath regarded the low estate of His handmaiden . . . He hath exalted them of low degree, and hath filled the hungry with good things " (i. 48–53). Parables also which are peculiar to this Gospel, and notably those of the Rich Man and Lazarus and the Rich Fool, teach the same lesson, the peril of riches and the blessedness of the poor.

(6) *The Gospel of Holy Joy*—Finally, St. Luke's Gospel is overflowing with gladness and thanksgiving. It is essentially the Gospel of Christian joy, a Gospel in which the leading personalities are ever singing and praising God. Zacharias, the Blessed Virgin, and Simeon give expression to their emotions in song. The word "joy" and its derivatives and correlatives occur with startling frequency in the Gospel. Zacchæus received our Lord "joyfully"; the shepherd brought home the lost sheep "rejoicing" and would have all his friends and neighbours "rejoice" with him; there is "joy" in the presence of the angels of God over one sinner that repenteth; "let us eat and make merry" is the father's welcome to the returned prodigal; and the Gospel closes on the same note of joy, "They returned to Jerusalem with great joy, and were continually in the temple, praising and blessing God."

Summary.—St. Luke's Gospel is in many respects the most attractive of the four Gospels and indeed of all the books of the New Testament. Nowhere else do we find such a delightful profusion and admirable blend of excellences. The Gospel of poetry, the Gospel of the woman, the Gospel of the poor, the Gospel of God's love for the sinner, the Gospel of Christian joy, these and other aspects of the message of our Lord Jesus Christ are set forth with such matchless literary art that a great writer like Ernest Renan, who was not particularly friendly to Christianity, declared the Gospel of St. Luke to be the most beautiful book in the world.

LECTURE V

THE GOSPEL ACCORDING TO ST. JOHN

You will have inferred from the tone of the previous lectures that the Fourth Gospel, as compared with the other three, stands in a class of its own and that it differs materially from these in the period to which it belongs, in its general character, and, more particularly, in its conception of the Person of our Lord Jesus Christ. It is this special character that the Gospel possesses which explains why we have had so little to say concerning it when we were dealing with the Synoptic Gospels and why it has to be given a place all to itself in our lectures.

There are two points of supreme importance in connection with the Fourth Gospel which we shall have to treat at some considerable length, viz.—

(1) Who wrote the Gospel?

(2) What value is to be attached to it as a historical document?

I propose to discuss the former of these two questions in the present lecture.

(A) THE AUTHOR OF THE FOURTH GOSPEL

St. John's Gospel is the only one of the four which contains any indication as to the identity of its author.

In xxi. 24 we read, "This is the disciple which beareth witness of these things, and wrote these things," and it is quite clear from the context that the disciple in question is he who is consistently described throughout the Gospel as "the disciple whom Jesus loved."

Again, in 1 14 and 1 St. John 1. 1 (assuming for the moment that the Gospel and the Epistle are by the same hand) we have a claim that the author is an eyewitness of the events he is describing.

Finally, in xix 35, after the description of the lance-thrust and the pierced side, the narrator adds the following statement : "And he that has seen this has borne witness, and his witness is true and *he* knoweth that he saith true, that ye may believe," where the *he* in italics seems to refer to the writer himself.

Now tradition from very early days identified "the beloved disciple" who is given such a prominent place in the Gospel with St John the Apostle, the brother of James and the son of Zebedee, and the Gospel has, therefore, been generally attributed to that Apostle.

I *External Evidence* —The following extracts from early Church writers give a clear idea of the views that were held with regard to the authorship of the Fourth Gospel towards the end of the second and the beginning of the third century.

Irenæus (writing about A D. 180), who was Bishop of Lyons in Gaul, but was a native of Asia Minor and acquainted, therefore, with Eastern as well as with Western tradition, writes : " John, the disciple of the Lord, who also leaned upon His breast, himself also published the Gospel, while he was dwelling at Ephesus, and he remained in the Church of Ephesus till the time of Trajan." (Quoted by Eus , *H E*., v. 8.)

Polycrates, Bishop of Ephesus and a contemporary of Irenæus, is also quoted by Eusebius (*H. E* , iii. 31) to the following effect : " Moreover, John, he that reclined on the bosom of the Lord, who as priest wore the sacred plate (τὸ πέταλον), martyr (μάρτυς) and teacher, he too

ST. JOHN 83

fell asleep at Ephesus." Although the Gospel is not specifically mentioned in this extract, it is clear that Polycrates was acquainted with it and that he was of opinion that the John who slept at Ephesus was its author. The allusion to the golden high-priestly frontlet that he associates with St. John is also of interest.

Theophilus of Antioch, who wrote about the same period (A.D. 180–190), quotes from the Gospel as the work of St. John. These are his words: " One of them, John, says, ' In the beginning was the word' " (*ad Autolyc.*, II. 22).

Clement of Alexandria, who wrote perhaps twenty years later than Irenæus, speaks thus of the Gospel: " John, perceiving that the bodily or external facts had been set forth in the (other) Gospels, at the instance of his disciples and with the inspiration of the Spirit, composed a spiritual Gospel," and he produces this statement as representing what he had learnt from the " early presbyters " whose memory might well go back to the lifetime of St John. (Quoted by Eus., *H. E.*, VI. 14.)

Origen, who flourished during the first half of the third century, is also cited by Eusebius as saying: " What must be said of the John who reclined on Jesus' breast ? He who has left one Gospel with the avowal that he could write far more than the world itself could contain " (*H. E.*, VI. 25).

Eusebius himself makes the following comment concerning the Gospel and its origin.

" The three Gospels first written having been by this time distributed everywhere and having come into John's hands, they say that he accepted them, bearing witness to their truth, but adding that there was only wanting to their record the narrative of what was done by Christ at first and at the beginning of His preaching."

The historian then adds that the Apostle John, being entreated to undertake the task of filling in these omissions, wrote an account of the period not touched on by the other Evangelists and of doings of the Saviour which these had failed to put on record. (*H. E.*, iii. 24.)

The Muratorian Canon.—Testimony to the Johannine authorship of our Gospel is also forthcoming even earlier than the time of Irenæus The Muratorian Canon, which gives a list of the books of the New Testament and is generally dated about the year 170, not only asserts that John, whom it describes as one of the disciples, wrote the Gospel, but also gives a detailed history of its origin which is interesting and well worth quoting. The following is the quotation · "At the entreaties of his fellow-disciples and his bishops, John, one of the disciples, said, 'Fast with me for three days from this time, and whatsoever shall be revealed to each of us (whether it be favourable to my writing or not), let us relate it to one another.' On the same night it was revealed to Andrew, one of the Apostles, that John should relate all things in his own name, aided by the revision of all. . . . What wonder is it then that John so constantly brings forward Gospel phrases even in his Epistles, saying in his own person, what we have seen with our eyes and heard with our ears and our hands have handled, these things have we written ? For so he professes that he was not only an eye-witness, but also a hearer, and moreover a historian of all the wonderful works of the Lord "

There is during the whole of this period under review only one voice raised which is in conflict with what is stated in the preceding extracts. An obscure sect to which Epiphanius gives the name of *Alogi*, attributed the authorship of the Fourth Gospel to the heretic Cerinthus.

ST. JOHN

You will have noticed that none of the writers quoted, with the exception of Eusebius, speaks explicitly of the author of the Gospel as John the Apostle, although the context in Theophilus almost certainly implies this. The common designation is John the disciple, but it is now generally agreed that the John whom Irenæus, Clement of Alexandria, and Origen had in view was the Apostle of that name.

It is now pertinent to ask what conclusion we are entitled to draw from the evidence that has been cited. If it is too much to assert, as some authorities do, that from the last quarter of the second century the Gospel was universally and without hesitation received as the work of the Apostle John, who composed it at Ephesus in his old age after the publication of the other three Gospels, there is no difficulty in accepting the more cautious verdict of a recent writer which runs as follows: " Before long time had elapsed it was generally, not universally, regarded as the work of one who, albeit not thus expressly designated, was nevertheless so alluded to as to indicate his identification with the Apostle John. And further the opinion was widespread that his home was in Asia Minor " [1]

It is also clear that there was current in that age a definite impression concerning the Evangelist's special purpose in putting forth another Gospel in addition to the three already in existence. The other Gospels had done justice to the outward facts and incidents in the life and ministry of the Lord, but it was St. John who wrote a Gospel that adequately represented the spirit and inner meaning of that wonderful life. Clement of Alexandria aptly expresses the idea dominant in his day concerning the true character of the Fourth Gospel when he designates it " the spiritual Gospel."

[1] Latimer Jackson, *The Problem of the Fourth Gospel*, p 26.

86   THE FOUR GOSPELS

This tradition concerning the authorship of the Gospel and its purpose held absolute sway in the Christian Church for sixteen centuries and remained unchallenged until the close of the eighteenth century, when an English clergyman named Evanson, who was vicar of Tewkesbury at the time, bluntly asked "how any kind of delusion should have induced creatures endowed with reason so long to have received the Fourth Gospel as the word of truth and the work of an Apostle of Jesus Christ?" From that time down to our own day no question connected with the New Testament has been so continuously and so fiercely discussed as the truth of the tradition that the Fourth Gospel is the work of St John, the Apostle and the son of Zebedee. Opinion in our own country is still on the whole in favour of the familiar view, but on the Continent and in America it is difficult to quote the name of any scholar of first rank, with the notable exception of Zahn, who now accepts the Gospel as the work of St. John.

The date of the Gospel.

Although the problem of the actual authorship still remains unsolved, recent criticism shows a gratifying tendency in one direction, viz. in the matter of the date of the Gospel. It happens rarely now that any scholar of standing places the writing of the Gospel so late as to preclude the possibility of its having been written by the Apostle St. John. Some sixty years or more ago the well-known German scholar, Baur, attempted to prove that the Gospel could not have been written before the middle of the second century, because, in his opinion, it showed manifest signs that its author was acquainted with several Gnostic heresies which were not in existence before that period. But a greater scholar than Baur, Bishop Lightfoot, gave that theory a decent burial,

ST. JOHN

and it is not likely to be disinterred in the near future. Lightfoot's prophecy uttered more than thirty years ago that "we may look forward to the time when it will be discreditable to the reputation of any critic for sobriety and judgment to assign the Gospel to any date later than the end of the first or the beginning of the second century" has been fulfilled almost to the letter.

There is no longer, therefore, any real difficulty with respect to the period in which our Gospel first saw the light, and we shall not go far astray if we adopt the years 90 and 110 as the *termini* between which the writing of the Gospel falls. The existence of the Gospel in the last decade of the first century does not prove of necessity that St. John was the author, but it does render the Johannine authorship possible if the tradition that the Apostle died at Ephesus when he was about a hundred years old is true. Baur's dating of the Gospel, on the other hand, put the traditional theory entirely out of court, so that the fairly general acceptance of a much earlier date for the Gospel is, as far as it goes, favourable to the view that it was the work of St. John.

Some difficulties associated with the external evidence.—We have seen that the Fourth Gospel from the year 180 was almost universally regarded as the work of St. John the Apostle, and that Theophilus of Antioch as early as 170 directly and explicitly attributes the Gospel to the Apostle. The real difficulty associated with the ascription of the Gospel to St. John belongs, however, to the period that elapsed between its publication and the time when it began to be received without hesitation as an Apostolic and Johannine document. To put the matter succinctly, the question that we are called upon to decide is whether Theophilus was justified by fact in describing the Fourth Gospel as the work of the Apostle John and whether the tradition of the Church from his time onwards was true to the previous history of the Gospel.

The history of the Gospel during that phase of its existence which preceded its general reception as a Johannine document is briefly as follows—

Taking as our evidence the writings of Clement of Rome, Ignatius, and Polycarp, the Didachè, the Epistle of Barnabas, the Shepherd of Hermas, the works of Justin Martyr, and extracts from Papias preserved by Eusebius, all of which were published between the years 90 and 155, and in a chronological order roughly corresponding to the above, the following facts emerge.

The name of St. John is never once mentioned in connection with the Gospel, and all that we can gather from such traces of the Gospel as are to be found in this catena of writings is that it was known at that period, but apparently not so well known as the other three Gospels.

The writings of Clement, Ignatius, and Polycarp show that there was in existence in their day a body of thought and teaching corresponding to that contained in the Fourth Gospel, but can hardly be said to testify to the existence of the Gospel itself.

The later writings of the period in question take us, however, a considerable step further and do manifest an undoubted acquaintance with the Gospel

The external evidence, then, down to the year 155 proves that the Gospel had been in existence for some time and was fairly widely circulated, but it throws little light on the question of authorship

Between A D. 155 and 180, and perhaps as early as the year 160, Heracleon, a disciple of Valentinus, the Gnostic leader, wrote a commentary on the Gospel, which is in itself a sign that by that time it was regarded as an authoritative document, but Heracleon makes no

ST JOHN 89

addition to our knowledge concerning the actual writer of the Gospel.

Reviewing the external evidence provided by ecclesiastical writers who flourished between the years 90 and 250 we seem to arrive at the following broad results—

(1) Down to the year 155 we find evidence of the existence of the Gospel and of its fairly wide circulation.

(2) Between the years 155 and 180 the Gospel had come to be regarded as an authoritative work.

(3) From the year 180 onwards the Gospel is almost universally accepted as the work of John, who is, however, rarely described as the Apostle John, although the manner of reference seems to show conclusively that the John in the mind of the writers was the Apostle of that name.

Those who dispute the Johannine authorship of the Gospel allege that there are serious difficulties connected with the evidence we have been discussing which go far to discount its value and render it inconclusive. There are two factors in particular which are said to militate strongly against the traditional theory when the external evidence is carefully examined—

(1) It is claimed that a Gospel which was the work of an Apostle of St. John's eminence and reputation would have been proclaimed as his from very early days and would not have led an existence of comparative obscurity in the Church for close upon a century.

(2) It is also alleged that the tradition that St. John resided at Ephesus for a considerable period and died there at a very ripe old age towards the end of the first or the beginning of the second century is difficult to establish.

The objections to the truth of this tradition are of a twofold character—

(*a*) If the tradition concerning the Apostle's residence

is true, how is the complete silence of Clement of Rome, Ignatius, and Polycarp on this point to be explained?

The tradition is first found in Irenæus, who, speaking of the events of his boyhood which was spent in Asia Minor, states in the most positive manner that he can call to mind the very place where the blessed Polycarp taught and can remember how that bishop spoke of his intercourse with John and of what he had heard from others who had seen the Lord. The John that Irenæus has in mind here is almost unquestionably the Apostle St. John, who was identified by him with the "beloved disciple" who wrote the Fourth Gospel. It is maintained, however, that the writings of the three great Apostolic Fathers show that they knew nothing of this residence of St. John at Ephesus.

Clement of Rome is writing to the Church of Corinth because that Church had given offence by its treatment of the presbyters, and it is pertinently asked why Clement, who lived in far-distant Rome, should have interfered in the affairs of the Church of Corinth, if St. John, the Apostle and the great ruling authority in the Christian Church at that time, was living at Ephesus within comparatively easy reach

Ignatius writes a letter to the Church of Ephesus, but makes not the slightest reference to St. John, who, according to the tradition, had died at Ephesus less than twenty years before. He does mention St. Paul, who had been dead half a century or so.

Polycarp, who, according to the statement of Irenæus, was a disciple of St. John, when writing to the Church of Philippi makes no reference to his former teacher, but appeals to the example of St. Paul.

It is difficult to believe that Irenæus could have been mistaken in what is apparently a simple matter of fact, and, on the other hand, it is not easy to explain the

ST JOHN

complete silence of the three Apostolic Fathers if Irenæus' story is correct. It is just possible that Irenæus may be referring to another John, and not to the Apostle of that name. Tradition leads us to believe that there was a second John living in Asia Minor at this period, and Eusebius tells of the existence in his time of two tombs at Ephesus, both of which bore the name of John This second John is generally designated " John the Presbyter," and it may be that it was this John who was in the mind of Irenæus when relating the story about Polycarp

(b) Some scholars assert that there is forthcoming adequate evidence to prove that St John the Apostle was dead long before the Gospel could have been written.

Two writers, Philip of Side in the fifth century and Georgius Hamartolus in the ninth, claim that Papias stated in one of his books that John, along with his brother James, *had been killed by the Jews* It is questionable, however, whether we ought to attach any importance to the evidence of these two writers. They are late authorities and they are also both notoriously inaccurate and unreliable Dr. Moffatt, who accepts their statements as affording positive proof that Papias was actually responsible for this report of the early martyrdom of St John, admits that the reputation of Philip as an independent historian is not particularly high, while much of the work of Georgius Hamartolus is demonstrably inaccurate. The statement in question possibly had its origin in some remark of Papias which these two writers completely misunderstood. If a writer, who was so well known to Eusebius as Papias was, had put forth a statement which was so directly opposed to the tradition which was universally prevalent in the Church in his day concerning St. John, it is most difficult to understand why that historian made no reference to it or why it should not have been heard of before the fifth century. We may also add that many scholars of note who are consistent opponents of the traditional theory of authorship do not attach any weight to this alleged statement of Papias as supporting their position.

Two factors, based on the special character of the Gospel which point to the Apostolic authorship.

It may be useful at this point to mention two factors, based on the special character of the Gospel, which tell in favour of the Apostolic authorship

The difference between the Fourth Gospel and its three predecessors in many important details must have been realised as soon as that Gospel became generally known in the Church The Synoptic Gospels were already being read in the public services and their contents must have been perfectly familiar to every well-instructed Christian, by whom they were regarded as giving a true, but possibly incomplete, story of the life and teaching of our Lord. It is also manifest that the writer of the Fourth Gospel was well acquainted with the work of the Synoptists and that the peculiar character of his own Gospel is due, in some measure, to his knowledge of what was contained or omitted in the work of his predecessors. It is, therefore, natural to ask—

(1) Could any one who was not an authority of first rank, an Apostle and a member of our Lord's inner circle of companions, have ventured to put forth a Gospel which differed so materially from the Synoptic tradition now so firmly established in the Church, and entertain any hope that it would command a hearing and a friendly reception?

(2) Would the Church have accepted a Gospel, however outstanding its merits and excellences may have

ST. JOHN 93

been, which was so manifestly distinct in form and material from the Gospels which it already possessed and valued, unless it had behind it an authority of unexceptionable and unimpeachable character, an authority of even higher quality than that of the other three Evangelists?[1]

Some of those who refuse to see in the Gospel the hand of St. John do as a matter of fact allege that there is substantial evidence showing that between the years 155 and 180 there was considerable opposition to its acceptance as an Apostolic document It is maintained that a certain work of Hippolytus, a learned Roman who lived at the beginning of the third century, called " A defence of the Gospel according to St. John and of the Apocalypse," which is among a list of the writings of that author found on the back of his chair and still preserved in the Lateran Museum in Rome, was specially composed in order to demolish the arguments brought forward against the Apostolic authorship of the Fourth Gospel by the *Alogi* and their leader, Gaius.

But compared with the reception which was accorded to the Gospel by the Church at large the opposition of certain narrow coteries is of little account, and this all but universal acceptance of a Gospel which was so new in the matter of its content and so alien in its general character to what the Church valued most is difficult to understand unless it had behind it the irresistible weight of Apostolic authority. The external evidence, then, taken as a whole, in spite of one or two difficulties of a somewhat serious character, goes far to establish the truth of the traditional theory that the Fourth Gospel is the authentic work of St. John the Apostle.

II. *Internal Evidence.*—We will now proceed to inquire

[1] Nolloth, *The Rise of the Christian Religion*, p. 37.

what light the Gospel itself throws upon the question of its authorship.

(1) The identity of "the beloved disciple" with the Apostle St. John.

You will call to mind that the Gospel in more than one passage makes a direct claim to be the work of "the disciple whom Jesus loved" and that tradition from early days has identified this disciple with St John the Apostle. In support of this identification it is pointed out that while the Synoptic Gospels have much to say concerning John, the son of Zebedee, and of his close intimacy with Christ, the Fourth Gospel never once mentions him by name. But it does speak frequently of a "disciple whom Jesus loved," who seems in this Gospel to occupy the same prominent position in the inner circle of our Lord's immediate followers as John, the son of Zebedee, does in the other three. It is suggested that the diffidence of a high-souled man like St. John would account for the omission of his name from the Gospel and for the restrained allusions to the loved disciple. "He veils his identity, but emphasises his capacity to bear witness and leaves to the judgment and common sense of the whole Church the naming of the author of its last Gospel" [1]

(2) There are also in the Gospel several indirect indications which seem to suggest that the author is an eye-witness of what he is describing and that this eye-witness is none other than St. John the Apostle.

Among the passages which convey this impression we may note the following—

(a) *The story of the first call of the Apostles* (1 35–51). —In this primary group of our Lord's disciples, whose call is described with considerable detail, there are *five* members, Andrew, Peter, Philip, Nathanael, and an

[1] Nolloth, *The Rise of the Christian Religion*, p. 26.

ST. JOHN 95

unnamed disciple, who is a follower of the Baptist and a friend of Andrew, and the tone of the narrative seems to indicate that this silent spectator in the background is telling the story.

Who could this early disciple of our Lord, who was among the first of those who obeyed His call, and who was a friend of Andrew, Simon Peter's brother, have been if not John, the son of Zebedee?

(b) *The story of the Woman of Samaria* (iv. 1–42).— Here again the narrative seems to come from the hand of one who witnessed the meeting of our Lord with the woman of Samaria and who listened to their conversation. Sanday suggests that St. John had not gone away with the rest of the Twelve, but had remained with the Master and was seated a pace or two away, not wishing to intrude his presence, but eagerly drinking in all that passed between the Master and His listener.[1]

(c) *The story of Lazarus* (xi. 1–46).—There is a vividness in the way in which this story is told which stamps it as representing the recollections of one who had been present at the events of the day, who had moved freely to and fro among the members of the household of Lazarus, and had talked with them after the day was over. The narrator is some one who, like our Lord Himself, was on terms of the closest intimacy with Mary and Martha, and who fills the part as well as St. John?

(d) *The narrative of the events in the Upper Room* (xiii. 1–30).—The whole of this chapter betrays the intense emotions of one who had watched that strange scene with his own eyes, and the description of the two episodes of the feet-washing and the indication of the traitor is so graphic and lifelike that it can only have

[1] Sanday, *The Criticism of the Fourth Gospel*, p. 83.

come from one who shared to the full in the experiences of that never-to-be-forgotten night.

(3) The argument in favour of the Johannine authorship is also strengthened by the *wealth of detail* which is a very marked characteristic of the Gospel. The closest attention is paid by the author to time, persons, and places, and the many and varied characters which pass before us in the Gospel are portrayed with remarkable preciseness and richness of colouring And further, the geographical, historical, and political descriptions come from one who is familiar with the situation in Palestine as it existed in the first half of the first century. The fall of Jerusalem in A.D. 70 had entirely changed the character of Judaism in all its departments The Holy City itself and the Temple, the centre and the very heart of the Jewish religion, had been destroyed, but a careful study of the Gospel shows that what the writer has in mind is not the Palestine or the Judaism of the latter end of the first century, but of our Lord's own day, and that the Jerusalem and the Temple that he describes are the city with whose beloved streets he himself had been so familiar and the sanctuary in which he had so frequently worshipped The Gospel, then, comes from the hand of one who knew Judæa and Jerusalem as they existed before the great catastrophe of 70 and who speaks of these as he remembers them in those days when he walked with Jesus.

What the line of argument we have sketched sets out to prove is, first of all, that the author of the Gospel was a Jew, which no one disputes, then that he was a Jew of Palestine, and finally, that he lived through the events that he is describing, was a member of the inner circle of our Lord's disciples, and was none other than St. John, the Apostle and son of Zebedee.

ST. JOHN 97

Arguments against the Johannine authorship based on the internal evidence.

Those who attribute the Gospel to another hand than that of St. John are by no means prepared to allow that the internal evidence we have been discussing is as favourable to the traditional theory as might be supposed at first sight I propose to state the case from this point of view as it is worked out by its latest exponent, Dr. H. L Jackson, in a remarkably reasonable and persuasive work called *The Problem of the Fourth Gospel* (1918), pp. 32-48.

Beginning with the *self-testimony* of the Gospel to the identity of its author, Dr. Jackson is of opinion that it raises more riddles than it solves.

Taking the passages in question in order—

(1) i 14, "*We beheld His glory.*" The "we beheld" does not necessarily imply physical perception and might only mean the spiritual realisation of the glory of Christ. And even if the writer here is claiming to be an eye-witness he was not necessarily one of the Twelve

(2) xix. 35 This is admittedly one of the most difficult passages to explain in the whole Gospel. It is questioned by many whether it is the "beloved disciple," the eye-witness and Evangelist, who is speaking here. Even if we allow that it is the "beloved disciple" who is in question, he adopts a strange fashion of indicating that he is the author. Then again the appeal in the latter part of the verse, "and *he* knoweth that he saith true," to one who apparently is not himself and whose identity is veiled enhances the obscurity of the whole passage. Conjectures without number have arisen as to the identity of this *he*, and among them the suggestion that he is none other than the risen and ascended Lord. There is no reason to doubt that the

author of the Gospel figures in the verse, but it is very difficult to decide whether he is pointed to by others or whether the passage is only an oblique way of indicating himself

(3) The last chapter is now generally regarded as an appendix to the original Gospel which ended with xx. 31, and even if it be granted that the appendix is from the hand of the author, the last two verses are demonstrably later additions to the chapter. Taken in connection with the bulk of the chapter these verses amount to an express assurance that "the disciple which beareth witness of these things and wrote these things" was "the disciple whom Jesus loved." The "*we*" in the statement "we know that his witness is true," who are qualified to bear witness, are perhaps the Ephesian elders or the Ephesian Church itself. But these verses do little more than reflect the opinion of a later day than that of the writing of the Gospel, and it is quite possible that they may have been added because doubt concerning the authorship was already prevalent. In discussing the *indirect indications* in the Gospel pointing to the identity of the author, Dr. Jackson allows that it is clear that he was a Jew addressing himself to Gentile communities and that his diction has more in common with Palestinian learning than with the literature of Hellenistic Judaism, and that he was, therefore, probably a Jew of Palestine. In dealing with the question whether the author's knowledge of Palestine is sufficiently accurate to establish the fact that Palestine had been his birthplace and his home, he states that nothing in the way of geography has yet been discovered to show that the Evangelist is not drawing on his own personal acquaintance with Palestine, and especially with Jerusalem, but he does not speak so positively with regard to the Evangelist's knowledge of

ST. JOHN

political affairs He is charged with having perpetrated a glaring blunder when, in more than one passage, he describes Caiaphas as being "high priest that year," implying that he thought the high-priesthood was an annual appointment and not an office tenable for life. It is alleged that no Jew acquainted with Palestine could be capable of such a mistake, and that the writer, living in Asia, was misled by the appointment of Asiarchs every year. Dr. Jackson does not, however, regard this objection as vital and is inclined to think that the phrase "that year" need not necessarily mean that the Evangelist was under the impression that the high-priesthood was an annual office. It may have meant nothing more than "that fateful year," "that year of all years"

A difficulty is also raised with regard to the *discourses of our Lord* incorporated in the Gospel, and it is contended that even if it be granted that the Evangelist was an *eye-witness* he could not have been an *ear-witness*, because these discourses are certainly not *verbatim* reports of our Lord's teaching. We shall have more to say on this point when we come to discuss the historical value of the Gospel in our next lecture.

The identity of the "beloved disciple."

A further difficulty arises in connection with the identity of the "beloved disciple." There is an increasing volume of opinion which maintains that even if we can establish the fact that the Gospel is the work of an eye-witness of the events that he is describing, and of one who was an intimate companion of our Lord and is designated "the disciple whom Jesus loved," it by no means follows that this disciple and John the son of Zebedee, were one and the same person. We are told that in character, in social position, and in the matter of residence the "beloved disciple" differs fundamentally from St. John the Apostle, as the latter is portrayed in the Synoptic Gospels The impetuous, intolerant, and vindictive son of Zebedee has but few features in common with the "beloved disciple" of the Fourth Gospel, and it is difficult to recognise in the Galilean fisherman the man who has the *entrée* of the high-priest's palace, whose home and interests are apparently in Jerusalem and not in Galilee. On this point, then, it is alleged that the traditional theory breaks down hopelessly, because whoever the "beloved disciple" may have been he was certainly not John the son of Zebedee Now if the "beloved disciple" was not St John the Apostle, it becomes pertinent to ask, who was he? It is claimed by some that he was not a real man of flesh and blood at all, not a historical personage, but "the exquisite creation of a devout imagination and a type of the spiritual witness to Jesus" Among those who see in him an actual person, some identify him with St. Paul, some with Nathanael, some with Lazarus, while a great scholar like the late Dr. Swete saw in him the "rich young ruler" who after his primary refusal was brought back by the love of Christ and attached himself to the Master with a fervour and whole-heartedness which justified the Lord's immediate recognition of his worth

SUMMARY.—I have placed before you the arguments for and against the Johannine authorship of the Fourth Gospel with all the fairness of which I am capable, and what shall we say of the outcome? It is clear that there are real difficulties associated with ascribing the Gospel to St. John the Apostle, but I am by no means convinced that the objections raised against the traditional theory are of such a vital character that we must now

ST. JOHN

definitely turn our back upon it and seek for a solution of the problem in some other direction. It must be frankly confessed that the trend of the latest critical opinion is against finding in the Gospel an authentic work of St. John, but time may produce a reaction and we may yet find ourselves encouraged and justified in regarding this pearl among Gospels as coming from the hand of one who knew our Lord as no one else knew Him, and whose knowledge was the fruit of the most intimate fellowship with Him. My greatest difficulty in accepting the non-Johannine solution is that I can find no satisfactory answer to the question · " If St. John did not write the Fourth Gospel, who did?" Among those put forward as possible candidates for the authorship are the writer of " The Epistle to the Ephesians" (assuming that this is not a genuine Pauline letter), the author of " The Epistle to the Hebrews," St. Andrew, Aristion, John Mark, and John the Presbyter But I fail to see in any one of these, with the possible exception of the author of " The Epistle to the Ephesians," if that Epistle is really not St. Paul's, the writer of a Gospel of such a unique and sublime character as our Fourth Gospel, and I can do no better than close the lecture with an apt quotation from a recent writer. " The Johannine question is still in the forefront of those trials to faith and patience which form a large part of our present discipline." [1]

Note.—Bishop Gore in a sermon preached on December 14, 1919, made the following important statement with reference to the question discussed in this lecture : " For my own part I have been passing the last few months in studying again the question of the authorship of the Fourth Gospel and I feel profoundly convinced

[1] Nolloth, *The Rise of the Christian Religion*, p 25.

that it was, as tradition says, written by John the Apostle." The reasons which underlie this statement have been published at considerable length in the introduction to the Bishop's edition of *The Epistles of St. John* (J. Murray, 1920).

LECTURE VI

THE GOSPEL ACCORDING TO ST. JOHN (*continued*)

(B) THE HISTORICAL VALUE OF THE GOSPEL

I. *The relation of the historical value of the Gospel to the question of authorship*

OUR estimate of the historical value of the Fourth Gospel, although of necessity bearing some relation to the problem of its authorship, is not entirely dependent upon the view we take of that problem. The student who is thoroughly convinced that the Gospel is the authentic work of St. John the Apostle, will naturally find in it more historical material than he who believes that it is the work of a Christian who never saw and never listened to our Lord. But even if we were in a position to prove the Johannine authorship beyond all possible doubt, that would not necessarily imply that all that is recorded in the Gospel represents actual historical fact. It is still arguable that the Apostle, writing sixty or seventy years later than the period he is describing, may have been so materially influenced by his long experience of Christ and of the Christian Church and by the development of Christianity on its doctrinal side that he came to regard the interpretation of the event as of greater moment than the event, and to set the idea behind the fact on a higher plane than the fact itself. It was some such notion as this concerning the character and purpose of the Fourth Gospel that underlay the statement of Clement of Alexandria who pronounced it to be a " spiritual Gospel." It was the spirit and not the letter, the idea and not the fact, that were dominant in our Evangelist's conception of what form a Christian Gospel should take, with the result that in every instance the actual incident is recorded not for the sake of its own value, but because of the idea foreshadowed in that particular event. Thus, even if we admit that the Gospel came from the hand of the Apostle, we may still justifiably hold that a considerable proportion of its contents is the product of the lifelong meditation and experience of the writer. But, on the other hand, to maintain that the Gospel is not Johannine in origin by no means implies that it, therefore, possesses no historical value. There is no difficulty in imagining a Christian disciple composing a Gospel towards the end of the first century which was almost entirely based upon original documents belonging to an earlier generation, which documents were of unquestionable authenticity, and in this manner producing a writing possessing first-rate historical authority.

In adopting this procedure he would only be following in the footsteps of his predecessor, St. Luke, whose claim to have produced an historical Gospel is, on his own confession, only based on the fact that he brought to bear upon materials already in existence, the mind, discretion, and insight of the true historian.

The question of the actual authorship of the Gospel does not, then, settle in one direction or another the further question of its value as an historical document, and this latter point must, therefore, be decided on its own merits

II. *The differences between the Synoptic Gospels and the Fourth Gospel.*

It is frequently alleged by those who view all attempts at Biblical criticism with disfavour that to the unbiassed

ST. JOHN 105

reader the Bible presents few real difficulties and that most of the questions which have agitated the public mind in reference to the Bible during the last half-century are not inherent in the Scriptures themselves but have been gratuitously raised by the critics. But assuredly the critics are not to blame for the emergence of the problem whether the Synoptists or the Gospel of St John contain the more accurate and the more historical description of the life and Person of our Lord Jesus Christ. The difference between the portrait of Our Lord contained in the first three Gospels and that contained in the fourth is patent to the simplest reader, and our problem, therefore, lies upon the very surface of the New Testament and calls imperatively for a solution.

To pass from the study of the Synoptists to that of St. John's Gospel is to experience a change of historical and theological climate and to move into an atmosphere which is strange and unexpected. Instead of the plain, simple narrative of the earlier Evangelists, with its scarcity of comment we are lifted on to a plane of eternal thoughts and ideas. The birth stories and genealogies of St. Matthew and St Luke are replaced by the heavenly procession of the Eternal Word from the Divine Father. St. John (we shall use this title in the remainder of the lecture for the sake of convenience only) hardly mentions the homely life and business of Nazareth and Capernaum, but concentrates his attention on Jerusalem and its Temple, and the long discussions which were held in the vicinity of the latter. The Sermon on the Mount has entirely disappeared, and in its place we find the mystical and unfamiliar language of the "farewell discourses." Many of the most prominent characters in the Fourth Gospel have no place at all in the Synoptists, and it is in *St. John* only that we read of Nathanael, Nicodemus, Lazarus, and the man born blind.

THE FOUR GOSPELS

The *geographical* elements are also widely at variance in the two records. The Synoptists point to Galilee as being the main scene of our Lord's ministry and Jerusalem does not appear on the horizon until the very close of His work. In *St. John*, on the other hand, Jerusalem is from the very beginning the centre of interest, and at least *three* visits to the Holy City are found in the narrative.

The same variation is also discernible in the matter of *chronology*. While the Synoptists only allow *one year* for the ministry, St. John's narrative demands *three*.

In the matter of *incidents* many of the most characteristic events recorded by the Synoptists are ignored by St. John. There is no explicit mention of the Virgin Birth, or of the Baptism, Temptation, and Transfiguration of Christ, and the Agony in the Garden and the Ascension are not so much as referred to. The Cleansing of the Temple and the Call of the Disciples are placed in an entirely new setting, while the Eucharistic Teaching seems to be out of its right place.

But the contrast between the Synoptic and Johannine records reaches its climax in the matter of *doctrinal presentation*.

The Christ of St. John is no longer the wonderful Teacher and Healer, but the Eternal and revealed Son of God. We seldom read of the Kingdom of God, which in the Synoptic Gospels is the central subject of His teaching, and in its place we have the most remarkable emphasis upon the Person of Christ, His eternal attributes, His pre-existence, and His mission to reveal the Father and through His own humanity to lift men into fellowship with God. He speaks no longer in parables, but in long discourses on mystical themes, and discussions of abstract terms like light, life, flesh,

ST. JOHN

glory, grace, and truth, have displaced the homely pictures of nature and simple daily life from which He draws His moral teaching in the earlier Gospels Miracles are also treated by St. John in a manner all his own. They are no longer works of mercy and loving-kindness towards a suffering and sin-stricken humanity, but every miracle has become a "sign" of deep significance, foreshadowing the glory of God and the Majesty of the Divine Son. Most significant of all, while the earlier Gospels represent our Lord as only very gradually unfolding His Messianic claims, St John from the very first sees in Him the Divine Son of God come in human flesh. "The Word was made flesh" is the keynote of his Gospel from its very commencement.

III. *Which of these two conceptions of the Life and Person of our Lord, the Synoptic and the Johannine, is the more true to historical fact?*

When we have once realised the significant contrast between the two types of record represented by the Synoptists and St John respectively it becomes natural to ask which of the two contains the more historical presentation of the life and teaching of our Lord. The first three Gospels, in spite of considerable differences in detail, clearly belong to the same literary family they tell the same story and portray the one and the same life The same point of view is common to all three, and comparing the story as told by the Synoptists with the record of St. John it is difficult to resist the conviction that, from the purely historical point of view, the former gives the truest representation of the facts. It gives an account of Christ's life and teaching which is natural and life-like and commends itself as presenting a true picture of Jesus of Nazareth as He lived and moved among men.

H

It would appear, then, that we are driven to conclude that if we are seeking for a conception of our Lord's life and Person which is true to ascertained fact we must turn to the Synoptic Gospels. But on the other hand, it would seem to be equally imperative that, if what we desire is a conception of our Lord as He is in very essence and as He revealed Himself to His Church, we have recourse to the Gospel of St. John. The difference between the two presentations is that between the photograph, accurately perhaps but somewhat mechanically reproducing the features, and the impressionist portrait, which reveals the very character and spirit of the subject.

IV *If this conclusion is correct, how much value are we to attach to St. John's Gospel as an historical document ?*

The old method of dealing with this problem, which was that of the Church for close upon eighteen centuries, was to assert that both records were historical and founded on fact. It was admitted that there were difficulties in reconciling the two presentations, but that there was no difficulty which reasonable scholarship could not remove, and certainly none of sufficient significance to cast any doubt upon the historical accuracy of the Fourth Gospel This was the view of scholars of the rank of Lightfoot and Westcott, and for that reason alone, if for no other, it deserves respectful treatment. On the other hand, you have a body of scholars who take quite a different view of the character of the Gospel and contend that it represents theology and not history, poetry and not prose. This is the standpoint of the great majority of continental scholars, and many of our own at home are in substantial agreement with them. It is argued by those who represent this view that there is no way of reconciling the two

ST. JOHN

portraitures of our Lord, and consequently, that, if the Synoptic record be accepted as true to the facts, the Gospel of St. John must be relegated to the sphere of the comparatively imaginary and can, therefore, be of little value as a source for the history of Christ There is, however, a third way of regarding the problem, which stands midway between the old traditional position and that of the Modernist, and it is in this direction that I am inclined to look for the solution of our problem. It is, I consider, quite clear that St. John's Gospel, taken as a whole, is not as strictly historical in its character as the other three, but it is an exaggeration to describe it as a purely theological treatise, in which facts and discourses have been manufactured by the author for a special purpose of his own. The view that I have mentioned above, which represents a compromise between the two extreme theories, is gaining ground rapidly among scholars of standing in our own day and is in a fair way of being firmly established as the truest and best explanation of the situation. We shall do well to bear in mind two all-important facts when we compare the Synoptic tradition with the Johannine.

(1) St. John's Gospel was written considerably later than the other three, and there is little room to doubt that the fourth Evangelist was well acquainted with the writings of his predecessors.

(2) It is demonstrable that the course of time and the development of Christianity on its many sides have exercised a palpable influence on St. John's conception of the life, teaching, and Person of our Lord Jesus Christ.

V *Elements in St. John's Gospel which reveal the influence upon the author of the age in which he lived.*

The following elements in the Gospel will serve to show the extent to which St. John was influenced by the natural growth and development of the Christian religion during the second half of the first century.

The *emphasis on the Second Coming of Christ* on the clouds of Heaven, which was such a fundamental constituent of the teaching of the first generation of Christians, is *absent* from our Gospel. It is the Christ in the heart of the believer that is the Christ to come according to St. John.

The *influence of St. Paul* is discernible on all the main doctrinal positions adopted by the fourth Evangelist, and it is not difficult to trace most of his significant ideas to their source in the teaching of the great Apostle of the Gentiles

The *wide Hellenistic world* with its rich culture, and more especially the great city of Alexandria and its particular contribution to Hellenistic thought, have left their mark upon both the form and the contents of the Gospel. Heretical doctrines, unknown to the earlier Evangelists and mainly of a Gnostic character, had already begun to make their presence felt in the Church, and these have had their share in forming the vocabulary and ideas of the Gospel.

But the influence of a growing and developing Christian consciousness is to be seen chiefly in an *enlarged and enriched conception of the character and functions of Christ*. The Synoptic Messianic idea, which was largely Jewish in origin and type, and, therefore, national and limited, is now replaced by the " Logos " doctrine which had its affinities in Greek philosophy. St. Paul had already recognised the inadequacy of the Jewish Mes-

ST. JOHN

sianic conception to represent the full significance of Christ, and in *St. John* the Pauline development reaches its climax in a conception of Christ which has now entirely outgrown its narrow Judaic environment and makes its appeal to the great Græco-Roman world.

Greater emphasis is also now placed *upon the spiritual and the Divine in Christ* than was done in the Synoptic Gospels. Those who had lived and walked with Jesus on earth had now reached the end of their course, with the possible exception of the Evangelist himself, and the physical bond which connected Christ with His disciples had been entirely broken For this outward bodily intimacy with our Lord an inward bond had to be substituted, and it was urgent in the interests of those who had not seen the Lord and yet had believed that the Church should be brought to realise that the inward fellowship with Christ was even more intimate and more real than that which was based on mere outward knowledge of Him. To impress this truth firmly upon the consciousness of the Church is one of the main objects of the Evangelist. On the other hand, no Christian writer ever exercised more care than St John *to define the true humanity of Christ* and to make it clear that the Christ who was believed in and adored was none other than Jesus, the Man, who had been seen and known in the flesh. It was his special function to teach that Christianity was no mere misty philosophy, but a personal religion founded on an historical Person, on Christ who lived, died, and rose again the third day. There is no hint in the Gospel to encourage the idea which has received a considerable amount of support in some quarters, that Christ was not an historic personage and that Christianity from its earliest beginnings has been founded on a myth.

The Gospel also bears other traces of the particular age to which it belongs, and more especially in the matter of the *controversies and discussions* which constitute a very considerable proportion of its contents. We note that our Lord's opponents are no longer any definite party or sect among the Jews, the Pharisees, Sadducees, or Herodians, as in the Synoptists, but that the whole Jewish nation is ranged against Him. The subject matter of the controversies is also different. The questions at issue are not in the main concerned with the Law and its observance or with the Messianic claims of Christ, and the opposition to Him is in this Gospel based upon the more abstract doctrines that He preaches, such as His relation to God, His claim to pre-existence, and His Eucharistic teaching. It is quite clear that what the Evangelist has chiefly in view are not the disputes between our Lord and the Scribes and Pharisees, but the hostility of Judaism as a whole to the Christian Church towards the end of the first century.

Finally, the *unquestionable acquaintance with Gnostic heresies* which the Gospel displays helps us to identify the period to which the Gospel belongs and the influences which were working upon the Evangelist. The great Gnostic ideas are frequently touched upon and some of the most characteristic and technical Gnostic terms, such as " light," " life," and " knowledge," are constantly in evidence. We should note, however, that if the terminology of the Gospel has affinities with Gnosticism the doctrines expounded are in all cases Christian and Catholic.

VI. *The relationship between St. John's Gospel and the Synoptic Gospels.*

We have already called attention to the fact that St. John was well acquainted with the work of his three predecessors and that he has made use of all the Synoptic Gospels. And we may go further and state that he has

ST. JOHN

treated the Synoptic Gospels as one who was in possession of fuller and more accurate information on some matters than was possessed by the other Evangelists He also, like St. Matthew and St. Luke, utilised St. Mark's narrative as a frame-work, but he has filled it in in a manner all his own Instead of Galilee Jerusalem is for him the centre of Christ's ministry He has also made a careful selection of the incidents related by the Synoptists, and in this matter of selection the numbers *three* and *seven* play an important part. Thus, *e. g.*, he relates seven miracles, and every miracle is a "sign" setting forth some fundamental principle, and in most cases the narrative describing the miracle leads up to a long discourse in which this particular principle is further expounded. And what is true of the miracles applies to practically every incident of our Lord's ministry that is given a place in the Gospel. It is not the event itself, but the event as a symbol of religious ideas that is significant for the Evangelist, and it is in this particular point of view that we find the explanation of the Evangelist's independent attitude towards the other three Gospels

The following details will illustrate how St. John has dealt with the work of his predecessors.

(1) He has *added* very substantially to our store of knowledge by placing on record several incidents which are not found in the Synoptic Gospels. Among this new material is to be found the miracle in Cana, the conversations with Nicodemus and the Woman of Samaria, the healing of the paralytic at Bethesda, and the raising of Lazarus. Some of these incidents and personages may not be as fresh as might appear at first sight. It is possible that Nicodemus may be the same as the young ruler of St. Mark x. 17 and St Matt. xix. 16. Echoes of the miracle in Cana may be found in

St Mark ii. 19, 22, " Can the sons of the bridechamber fast while the bridegroom is with them ? " and the story of the paralytic may be only another version of the healing of the " man sick of the palsy " at Capernaum

(2) St. John has *omitted* from his Gospel several of the most characteristic incidents chronicled by the Synoptists, such as the Baptism, the Temptation, the Transfiguration, the Institution of the Eucharist, the Agony in the Garden, and the Ascension. There is no real difficulty in understanding why the Evangelist omitted these particular incidents. When we have once realised what his characteristic conception of the Person of Christ was, the reason why he found no place in his narrative for these events is quite simple. St. John sets our Lord before his readers in the perfection of His Manhood and in the completeness of His Godhead. " The Word was made flesh " is the text of his discourse from beginning to end, and the Jesus who lived with His disciples is never other than the Eternal Son of God. It is this conception of Jesus as the Son of God that explains the omission of such incidents as the Baptism, Temptation, and the Agony in the Garden from his record These might be interpreted in such a way as to impute weakness or subordination to Christ and might, consequently, be regarded as derogatory to the Divine power and majesty of the Incarnate Word. Again, in St John's mind there was not a moment in the earthly life of Christ when He was not surrounded with all the glory of Heaven, and there was, therefore, no room for an incidental Transfiguration. There is no Ascension in the Gospel because Jesus had never ceased to be the Eternal Son.

(3) The problem of the *discourses* in the Fourth Gospel is probably the greatest difficulty connected with it. The difference between our Lord's manner of teaching

ST. JOHN

as represented in the Synoptists and the discourses attributed to Him by St. John is apparently fundamental. In method, style, and substance we seem to be met by two entirely different entities. The parable, which is practically our Lord's one and only method of instruction in the Synoptic record, has completely disappeared and in its place we find long speeches so composed that it is frequently a matter of the greatest difficulty to tell where our Lord's words end and those of the Evangelist begin. And again, every one in the Fourth Gospel speaks exactly in the same style, our Lord Himself, Nicodemus, Nathanael, Martha and Mary, as well as the Evangelist, so that we are irresistibly led to the conclusion that we have not in these discourses a *verbatim* report of our Lord's utterances but a reconstruction of our Lord's teaching in the Evangelist's own style and language The substance of the discourses differs as widely from that of our Lord's teaching as represented in the Synoptists as do their method and style Instead of such subjects as the Kingdom of Heaven, the Fatherhood of God, and the ethical truths of the Sermon on the Mount, our Lord's teaching in St. John is centred wholly upon Himself. To define the relationship existing between the Synoptic and the Johannine types of teaching is, therefore, a very real problem To say that the discourses in the Fourth Gospel are the product of free invention, which is the solution propounded by some modern critics, does not fit in with a reasonable conception of the character of the Evangelist or of the Gospel, and to suggest that St. John is drawing upon a tradition unknown to the Synoptists, as the more conservative critics do, does not seem to be substantially nearer the mark.

A more satisfactory solution is contained in the hypothesis that the Johannine discourses are ultimately based on material which is actually present in the Synoptic Gospels. It is an undeniable fact that there are few Johannine utterances to which parallels are not available in the other Gospels. What St. John has done is to expand the Synoptic teaching, change its emphasis, and reconstruct the actual language in order to bring out more fully the inward idea. An excellent illustration of this method may be found in the discourse with Nicodemus, which is after all only an expansion of St. Matt. xviii. 3, "Except ye be converted and become as little children ye shall not enter into the Kingdom of Heaven," and this is true in a greater or lesser degree of most of the Johannine teaching concerning the Person of Christ. Dr. Nolloth,[1] whom we have frequently quoted before, is of opinion that a case may be made out for the contention that the Johannine discourses do actually represent our Lord's own utterances. He considers that the reason why St. John only has preserved those discourses of our Lord which are in dialogue form was his special fondness for the dialogue. He also suggests that St. John, as "the disciple whom Jesus loved," would probably be in our Lord's company when the others were away, and so may have overheard the conversations with Nicodemus and the Woman of Samaria which he alone has recorded. The High-Priestly Prayer he reproduced because he alone was able to enter into its meaning and to retain it in his memory. In the repeated assurance of the Evangelist's special nearness to the human heart of Jesus, Dr. Nolloth sees the explanation of his capacity to narrate what was most intimate and reserved in the Master's utterance and not a mere boast of privilege. Love was here the key to knowledge. This is satisfactory as far as it goes, but it does not explain why every one in the Gospel

[1] Nolloth, *The Rise of the Christian Religion*, p. 30.

ST. JOHN 117

speaks in this peculiar style, and we are, it seems to me, still driven to conclude that the Johannine discourses do not represent the actual utterances of our Lord, but a reconstruction of those utterances by the Evangelist himself.

(4) There are three instances where the Fourth Gospel is *directly at variance* with the Synoptists, viz. ·

(a) The length of the ministry.
(b) The number of the visits to Jerusalem.
(c) The date of the Crucifixion.

The tendency of recent criticism is to assign a greater degree of accuracy to St. John than to the Synoptists in all three cases. The notion that our Lord's ministry only covered one year and that He only paid one visit to Jerusalem, and that at the very close of His earthly career, is ultimately based on St. Mark's narrative, but there are hints in Q which seem to substantiate the view that the ministry lasted for more than two years and that our Lord visited Jerusalem on several occasions during that period. With respect to the date of the Crucifixion, opinion is slowly but surely turning in favour of the Johannine position, which means that our Lord was crucified not on the fifteenth, but on the fourteenth of Nisan, and that the Eucharist was, therefore, instituted on the night before the Passover and not on the night of the Passover itself.

(5) Finally, there are three incidents recorded in the Gospel *concerning whose historicity grave doubts have been expressed* by scholars who are by no means extreme in their views.

(a) *The Cleansing of the Temple* —Here St. John seems to have misplaced the incident. The sequence of events in the Synoptists, where this is put at the close of the ministry and not at its opening, as in St. John, is certainly more natural and true to life. In the Synoptic record it forms one of the main causes of the hostility of the Jewish hierarchy towards Jesus and leads indirectly to His arrest, trial, and death. It is possible, however, that the misplacing is due to the Synoptists and not to St. John. If the cleansing of the Temple did take place at Jerusalem early in the ministry the other Evangelists, who are tied to one visit only to the Holy City, would have no option but to connect the incident with that one visit.

(b) *The Institution of the Eucharist.*—St John, though apparently giving a detailed account of the events in the Upper Room, entirely ignores the institution of the Eucharist and connects the Eucharistic teaching of Christ with an early Galilean miracle, the feeding of the five thousand. There are traces, however, even in the Synoptic narrative of this miracle of a simple Eucharistic idea, and the language has a liturgical colouring. It is, therefore, possible that while the Last Supper was the normal and central embodiment of Eucharistic ideas it was not the only embodiment, and that the association of Eucharistic teaching with the miracle of feeding was not due to the initiative of St John, but represents historical fact.

(c) *The Raising of Lazarus.*—This is the greatest of all the difficulties in connection with the historicity of the Gospel. An exceedingly sane and fair-minded critic like Dr Burkitt writes as follows on this point: " The discrepancy between the Fourth Gospel and the Synoptic narrative comes to a head in the story of Lazarus. It is not a question of the impossibility or improbability of the miracle, but of the time, and place, and effect upon outsiders. There is no room for the miracle in St Mark. If the event was so public as St. John insists, so fraught with influences upon friends and foes, it could not have been unknown to a well-informed

ST. JOHN 119

personage like St. Mark, and there is no reason for suppressing a narrative so public and so edifying. St. Mark is silent about the raising of Lazarus because he did not know of it, and, therefore, because it ·never occurred "[1] Other scholars use similar language in criticising the story. Their view is that St. John's narrative is a dramatised version of the Lucan parable, "The Rich Man and Lazarus," helped out by certain borrowings from St. Luke x, where Mary and Martha are introduced into the context I am not convinced, however, that Dr. Burkitt is justified in laying so much stress upon the silence of St Mark or in claiming so positively that that Evangelist could not possibly have ignored the miracle if he had known of it. He had already placed on record one such raising of the dead by Jesus, and he may have considered that this was quite adequate for his purpose.

Summary.—It is, in my opinion, tolerably clear that St. John, when he set out to write his Gospel, did not propose to compose a strictly historical document. His object was rather to explain and interpret the life and teaching of Christ, and that with the view of leaving a particular impression upon the soul of the Church of his own age His purpose is explicitly declared in xx 31 · " These are written, that ye may believe that Jesus is the Christ, the Son of God, and that believing ye may have life in His name."

This is the spirit and principle that account for his independent attitude towards the other Gospels and the additional material that was at his disposal. The facts that he chronicles are generally historical facts, and even where incidents are related apparently for the first time, something which is approximately like them is to be found in the Synoptists. Very frequently the

[1] Burkitt, *The Gospel History and its Transmission*, p. 221 f.

Johannine narrative is only a development and expansion of a hint contained in the work of his predecessors The discourses in style and phraseology are frankly Johannine, but even here the substance is often implicit in the Synoptists. The events of our Lord's life and the substance of His teaching are read in the light of a long Christian experience. In some respects we have found that the historical value of St. John's Gospel is superior to that of the Synoptists, and, on the whole, I am inclined to think that the Fourth Gospel contains more strict history than it is sometimes credited with, while I am perfectly convinced that any conception of the life, work, and character of our Lord Jesus Christ which does not take into account the Johannine record is woefully incomplete and inadequate. In point of spiritual value St. John's Gospel is unique and unapproachable, and it has, of all the Gospels, made the deepest impression upon the soul of the Christian Church.

FINIS.

ID# INDEX

Acts of the Apostles
  Date, 17, 18
  Story of St Mark in, 22-23
  Story of St Luke in, 59-64
  Women in, 78
Alogi, 84, 93
Beloved disciple, identity of, 94, 99-100
Christ
  Place of, in life of to-day, 2-4
  in *St Mark*, 31-36
  in *St Matthew*, 44, 45, 49-50, 51, 53, 54
  in *St Luke*, 71, 74-79
  in *St. John*, 106, 110, 111, 114
Church, the
  Early Church and the Gospels, 4-9
  in *St Matthew*, 56-57
  and *St John*, 92-93
Eschatology, 7, 55, 56
Ethics, Christian, 57-58
Gnosticism, 112
Gospel, unwritten, 5-6
Gospel of St Mark
  Its priority, 13-15
  Relation to *St Matthew* and *St Luke*, 13, 15, 16
  Date of, 17, 18
  Place in New Testament, 19, 20
  Authorship of, 21-24
  Connection with St. Peter, 24-29
  History of, in early centuries, 29-30
  Contents and special characteristics, 30-36

Gospel of St Matthew
  Relation to *St Mark* and Q, 13-16
  Date of, 16-18
  Place in New Testament, 19, 20
  Authorship of, 37-43
  Purpose of, 43-45
  Contents of, 45-47
  Its treatment of *St Mark*, 47-53
  Characteristic features of, 53-58
Gospel of St Luke
  Relation to *St Mark* and Q, 13-16
  Date of, 16-18
  Place in New Testament, 19, 20
  Authorship of, 59-65
  Purpose of, 65-67
  Sources of, 67-75
  Its treatment of *St Mark*, 68-70
  Its use of Q, 70-71
  Special features of, 75-80
Gospel of St John
  Place in New Testament, 19, 20
  Authorship of, 81-102
    External evidence for, 82-93
    Internal evidence for, 93-100
  Date of, 19, 86-87
  Historical value of, 103-120
    Difference from Synoptic Gospels, 104-107
    Strictly historical worth, 107-109

INDEX

Gospel of St John
    Signs of influence of later age, 110–112
    Relationship to Synoptic Gopels, 112–120
    Discourses in, 114–116
    Additions, omissions, and variations in, 113–119

Gospels, the
    Attraction of, 1–4
    Origin of, 4–9
    of the New Testament, 9–10
    Dates of, 16–19
    Order of, in the New Testament, 19–20
    Symbols of, 20
    Length of, 46–47

Gospels, Synoptic
    Mutual relations, 10–16, 29, 39–42, 45, 68
    Comparison with *St John*, 104–109
    Relationship to *St John*, 112–120

Gospels, Apocryphal, 9–10

John, St
    Residence at Ephesus, 88–91
    Alleged early martyrdom, 91–92

John the Presbyter, 91, 101

Kingdom of Heaven, the, 55–57, 106, 110

Logia, 39–43

Luke, St , his story, 59–65

Mark, St , his story, 21–24

Oral theory, the, 11–16, 67

Patristic evidence for Gospels, 8, 24–26, 29–30, 39–43, 62, 82–85 87–92

Paul, St
    Connection with St Mark, 21–24
    Connection with St Luke, 60–64, 74, 75
    Influence on St John's Gospel, 110

Peter, St
    Connection with St Mark, 21–24
    Connection with St Mark's Gospel, 24–29

Prophecy, Old Testament, in St Matthew, 53–55

Q
    Character and contents, 14–15
    Use in *St Matthew* and *St Luke*, 14–15
    Date of, 18
    Its use by St Matthew, 39–43, 45
    Its use by St Luke, 68, 70–71

Sermon on the Mount, the, 57–58, 70–71, 105

Synoptic Problem, the, 10–16, 29, 39–42, 45, 68

Women in St Luke's Gospel, 77–79

www.ingramcontent.com/pod-product-compliance
Lightning Source LLC
Chambersburg PA
CBHW070458090426
42735CB00012B/2599